TALES OF COURAGE, TALES OF DREAMS

A Multicultural Reader

JOHN MUNDAHL

Addison-Wesley Publishing Company, Inc.

Reading, Massachusetts • Menlo Park, California • New York
Don Mills, Ontario • Wokingham, England • Amsterdam
Bonn • Sydney • Singapore • Tokyo • Madrid • San Juan
Paris • Seoul • Milan • Mexico City • Taipei

All selections were written by John Mundahl, unless otherwise noted.

Product Development Director: Judith M. Bittinger

Editorial: Elinor Chamas, Clare Siska

Production/Manufacturing: James W. Gibbons

Cover and Text design: Laura Fredericks

The designs used in this book were adapted from the folk motifs of ancient Mexico, Peru, Africa, Lapland, and Laos.

All illustrations by Hannah Bonner, except pp. iv and 38 by Nhat Dang, p. 32 by Vika Ivchenko, and pp. 56 and 61 by Philip Mundahl.

Text credits appear on page 157.

Library of Congress Cataloging-in-Publication Data

Mundahl, John, 1945–
    Tales of courage, tales of dreams : a multicultural reader / John Mundahl.
       p. cm.
    Includes bibliographical references and index.
    ISBN 0-201-53962-4 :
    1. Readers—United States.   2. United States—Ethnic relations—Problems,
exercises, etc.   3. Pluralism (Social sciences)—Problems, exercises, etc.
4. English language—Textbooks for foreign speakers.   I. Title.
PE1127.H5M8 1993
428.6'4—dc20

        92-42252

ISBN: 0-201-53962-4

4 5 6 7 8 9 10-CRS-97 96 95 94

Dedicated with love to my daughter, Becky

Rise and shine,
We are all children of the Universe
Clinging to a grain of sand
In the body of an infinite Universe,
Waiting to take a giant step.
Only together will we reach the stars
And find answers and see the mystery of life.

Red Bone
Native American

Acknowledgments

I would like to thank the following teachers in the Minneapolis Public Schools who graciously gave their time to read and comment on the manuscript: Olha Breslawec, Pat Budd, Rick Gresczyk, Shirley Krogmeier, Marilyn Lading, Pat Lee, Estelle Mount, Nancy Olson, Robert Reed, Kathy Runchey, Judy Strohl, and Wendy Weimer. Thank you to Ellen Baer, Suzanne Griffin, Charles Lindsay, David Moore, Pat Wilcox Peterson, Dennis Terdy, and Blair Wilson who also generously served as readers.

Thank you to Carol Compton and Tom Reynolds for their interest and encouragement, and to Charles Skidmore for generously sharing his students' work. Thank you to Mr. Soua K. Yang, Ha H. Tuong, Nhat Dang, Hai Nguyen, Samlong Inthaly-Smith, Allen Flying By, Kate Bresnahan, Bouy Te, and Rima Al-Azar who served as native language and cultural reviewers.

Thank you to Linda Moran and Dao Peter Yang for allowing me to tell the story of Joua Yang. Thank you to Maria Odermann, Halyna Ivchenko, and Vika Ivchenko for their help with Vika's story. Thank you to Elin Schultz for her ideas for plate hangings, wind socks, accordion books, and mobiles.

Thank you to my brother, Philip, for his faith in my writing ability, to William Olson, who encouraged me always, to my daughter, Becky, who sat on my lap while I typed, to Evelyn Nelson at Addison-Wesley who encouraged me to submit the manuscript, and to Judith Bittinger who accepted the manuscript. A special thanks to my two talented editors, Elinor Chamas and Clare Siska, who shaped the stories and the book in a beautiful manner, were gracious and constructive in their suggestions, and never tired in their desire for excellence.

And finally, thank you to the thousands of refugee and immigrant children and their families who have touched me with their courage and their dreams. May you find a new life here. May your tears turn to pearls.

John Mundahl
Minneapolis, Minnesota

To the Teacher

Tales of Courage, Tales of Dreams is a beginning/intermediate reader for older ESL students in grades 5-12. It is also appropriate for young adults.

Special Features of *Tales of Courage, Tales of Dreams*

1. Story ideas   The story ideas came from my work as an ESL teacher with refugee and immigrant students. Written specifically for ESL students, the stories represent many different cultures, including Mexican, Puerto Rican, Native American, Indian, Brazilian, Jamaican, Korean, Laotian, Cambodian, Vietnamese, Russian, Ukrainian, Haitian, Dominican, Nigerian, African American, Amerasian, Lebanese, Hmong, and the United States.

2. Reading Level   Most of the stories are written at a second or third grade reading level. Sentence length is short, difficult words are glossed, simple past tense is used as much as possible, and passive voice is avoided. Longer stories are divided into small, manageable parts that can be read over several sessions.

3. Themes   The stories are arranged thematically around eight major themes. Even though reading level is low, the themes are of interest to older students. Themes such as the destruction of the environment, loss of homeland, racial prejudice, adjustment to life in the United States, love, courage, triumph, starting over, and respect for other cultures are developed.

4. Use of Native Language   In many of the stories the characters speak in their native language. This gives students a chance to see their own language in an American reader. It also provides excellent springboards for discussions on language differences. The opening section of the book, "Tales of our Old and New Lives," contains actual student writings, presented just as they were written. These selections will encourage your own students to write about similar experiences.

5. *Values* Each story is centered around a value which is taught through the medium of the story. Non-violence, honesty, respect for the earth, love for homeland, compassion, simplicity, and other such values are developed.

6. *Responding to Reading* Each group of reading selections is followed by questions and activities to stimulate discussion, thought, and writing on the selections just read. In addition, each section concludes with suggestions for more reading on similar topics.

Suggestions for Teaching

1. Read the selections to the students while they listen. One way to begin a new selection is to set the historical or cultural background for the selection and then read the selection to the students while they follow along in their books. This allows the students to hear correct pronunciation and English rhythms. It also allows students to make contextual guesses at the meanings of new words.

2. Have the students read the selections:
   - ▲ silently by themselves. Students can read for understanding and pleasure without having to know the meaning or correct pronunciation of each word.
   - ▲ out loud in pairs. This is an unthreatening way to elicit speech. It also allows the whole class to be actively involved in the lesson at the same time and allows students to help each other with English pronunciation.
   - ▲ out loud in groups or while role playing. These methods for eliciting speech provide variety in your lesson plans.
   - ▲ at home to parents, grandparents, relatives, or siblings. This encourages other family members to become involved in the education of your students.

3. Put the selections on tape. Students can use the tapes as they practice reading and listening skills.

4. Have students keep a journal. In it, they can:
   - ▲ note difficult vocabulary or phrases,
   - ▲ keep a diary of their reactions to the stories,

▲ write the rough drafts of writing exercises,

▲ keep a log of how many times they read a selection and to whom.

5. Look for ways to compare cultures, learn about other cultures, and teach respect and tolerance for other cultures. Help your students become culturally conscious by comparing native languages, clothing, food, life-styles and values. The Multicultural Index on page 151 can help you locate selections based in specific cultures.

6. Include parents in the education of their children. Involve them and other family members by having students:

▲ conduct interviews,

▲ share and talk about family photographs and history,

▲ invite family members to class,

▲ read to and with their family at home,

▲ write letters to local or distant relatives,

▲ share their family's traditional clothes, food, or customs with the class.

7. Look for opportunities to connect any of the stories to content area classes, such as health, social studies, science, math, or English. Discussions of plot, character, setting, and theme prepare students for mainstream English classes. Historical or geographical information about a specific country, culture, and people help students in social studies classes. Stories in "Tales of Long Ago" connect well with literature studies. Stories in "Tales of the Earth" connect well with mainstream science classes.

8. Encourage your students to interact with the selections in as many ways as possible: speaking, listening, music, movement, writing, art, drama, dance, and storytelling exercises contribute to understanding and expand language skills. Remember the Chinese proverb: "I hear, I forget. I see, I remember. I do, I understand."

9. Allow students time to connect the themes to their own lives. The stories in each section of the book offer different slants or experiences of the same general theme for the section. In "Tales of Love," for example, each story depicts love in a different form: love between grandparent and grandchild, love as joy, love as comfort. Explore the major themes of the book in detail.

Suggestions for Group Activities

1. Big Books Big Books are popular with young children and can be used by older students as well. Older students can make their own big books using their favorite story selections. They can summarize a story using large print and add their own art work. These books can become a permanent part of your classroom, library, or resource room. Capitalization, punctuation, and the relationships between words can be especially highlighted as these books are created.

2. Plate Hangings This project increases comprehension by allowing each student to interact with a reading selection through the medium of art. It is a simple activity, requiring little proficiency in English. Use four small paper plates. On the first plate, write the title of the story. On the second plate, draw a picture from the beginning of the story. On the third plate, draw a picture from the middle of the story. On the fourth plate, draw a picture from the end of the story. Tie the plates together with string and hang them in class.

3. Wind Socks This is a creative activity that connects students to reading selections through art. Draw a major scene from a story on a 9-by-12-inch piece of paper. Staple the paper into a cylinder. On four 2-by-12-inch paper strips, write the title and sentences from the beginning, middle, and end of the selection. Staple the strips to the cylinder.

4. Accordion Books This is another art activity that increases comprehension by allowing students to engage in a reading selection with minimal comprehension of English. Fold a 4-by-18-inch paper twice to form an accordion. On each panel, draw a picture from a story. Include the story title.

5. Mobiles This activity provides students with a creative way to engage in a reading selection. Mobiles are excellent for studying plot, character, and setting, or for beginning writing activities.

They also add color to your room and hallways. Cut strips of paper. Tie them to a coat hanger. On the strips write about the plot, characters, setting, and theme of the story.

6. Collages   Make a poster about the selection using pictures, drawings, words, and sentences. Collages are excellent for eliciting oral speech and for introducing ESL students to American magazines and newspapers as they search for pictures and phrases. Collages add color to your room and give students an activity to show to parents.

7. Newspaper Articles   Look in newspapers or magazines for stories related to the selection you are studying. This is an excellent way to teach beginning research skills, knowledge of the sections of a newspaper, knowledge of magazines, and consumer awareness. It also encourages students to read at home and provides a fun activity in which to involve families.

8. Drama   Develop a selection into a play and present it for other students, family, or your community. Drama brings your class together. Preparation of a script encourages cooperation, oral speech, and meaningful writing. A reading selection is enhanced through the creation of a play when the written characters come to life in words and native dress.

9. Spelling Challenge   Divide into teams. Have each team choose ten words from a selection and challenge other teams to spell the words. This activity offers relief from classroom routine, encourages cooperative learning, and provides a fun, non-threatening opportunity for oral language.

10. Art   Draw pictures of favorite characters or action scenes from a selection. This can be done individually or as a group mural. This is a good opportunity for beginning ESL students to write simple captions and to talk about their pictures.

11. Grammar Search   Have students find examples in the selections of specific grammatical concepts they are studying. Students work individually, in groups, or in pairs. They write examples in their journals.

12. Hangman   Students play hangman in groups or pairs using words from the selections. This game provides spelling practice. You, as teacher, can also play and challenge the class.

13. Story Components   Discuss plot, setting, character, and themes of short stories. Discuss folktales, poetry, short biography, fiction and non-fiction. This will prepare students for mainstream English classes. The Literary Genre Index on page 153 can help you locate specific types of selections.

14. Storyboards   This is a bulletin board or display board which features the selection being read. Highlight plot, character, themes, setting, vocabulary, and anything else you feel is important or particular to the selection. A storyboard, often created by the students, helps focus the class on the selection, serves as a daily reminder of the selection being read, and provides a colorful way to emphasize important words, phrases, and cultural values found in it.

15. Word Finds   Create word finds from the selections, or have students make up their own. Students can look for words within words, words that share a common theme (food, sports, etc.), or words that are related in other ways. Word finds are useful as homework for beginners and are interesting to other family members as well. They provide a fun way to study vocabulary, spelling, and content.

16. Summaries   Advanced students can write summaries of the selections. This is particularly helpful to students about to be mainstreamed. Check for organization, accuracy of information, spelling, punctuation, and capitalization.

17. Letters   Write letters to favorite characters in the selections. Students might ask for advice, give an opinion, give support, share a similar experience, or ask for information. Letters can be read or kept confidential in student journals. They can be "answered" by someone else in the class pretending to be the character from the selection.

18. Alternative Endings   Have students write a different ending to a story. This allows students to draw upon their own life experiences, encourages creative writing, and heightens emotional involvement in the story.

19. Comprehension Questions   Have students write their own comprehension questions. This can be done as a game in teams or pairs. Each team challenges another team. This exercise is particularly useful when the class is studying *Wh-* questions or English interrogative patterns.

20. Charts   Have students chart each story in their journal. Use plot, characters, setting, theme, vocabulary, and cultural values as headings and have the students fill in the needed information. This teaches important study skills (gathering critical information, outlining, note-taking, etc.).

Table of Contents

Tales of Our Old and New Lives

When I stood at the airport in America,
Waiting for my uncle to pick me up,
I felt like a piece of sand in the desert.

Thanh-Tu Nguyen
Vietnamese

The Voices of Students

Life in a new country is different and exciting. Sometimes it is also difficult. There is a new language, new food, new school, new friends, and memories of home that will never go away. Sometimes you may feel caught between two cultures, a stranger to both. Read the words of these students. Then write down your own feelings. Do you share the same feelings as these young people?

▲▲▲▲▲▲▲▲▲▲

I fled, but I left my heart in my country.
I fled, but I still love Vietnam.
Oh! I will never forget.

Now I am in a foreign land
Trying to study for the future.
To pay tribute to teachers and parents
For raising me to become a man.

Their words are wide like sky and ocean.
I will keep them in my heart wherever I go.
But I still remember I am Vietnamese.

Thu Phan, Vietnamese

▲▲▲▲▲▲▲▲▲▲

I remember when I first came to the United States, there were a lot of things that seemed look great to me. It was summertime when I came here and it was very hot and humid. Then three months later I started going to school and that school was Southwest. The first thing I noticed was the fashion because in my country you have a uniform to go to school. Then the school bus, because we don't have school buses in my country. In my country you have your own books and here the teacher lets you borrow them until the end of the year.

I remember when I first started school, I was very happy and glad. Sometimes I was sad because I didn't have any friends but I have a lot of friends right now. For me it was exciting because I got use to my country then all of sudden I was here and everything was different.

Luisito Malinis

▲▲▲▲▲▲▲▲▲▲

When I read a book, I feel so empty, because even though I can read the words, I can't understand the content, because English is new to me. I'm trying to live my life in English, but it is frustrating because I know I'm missing so much.

Hyon Ju Scotton, Korean

▲▲▲▲▲▲▲▲▲▲

My first day in an American high school was terrible. I didn't know which room to go to. I didn't speak English. I couldn't talk to anyone, and I am a shy girl anyway. I walked in the hallway and saw all the Americans. I was afraid, and I couldn't understand a word. I went to class and sat in the corner.

The teacher gave the students five or ten minutes to discuss something. Everybody gathered with their friends and talked. I sat alone in the corner. Nobody asked about me or talked to me. One time I cried in class. Nobody knew it because I hid my tears. I tried not to cry, and told myself I had to learn English because my family had paid a high price for freedom, so I couldn't waste it.

When I wrote my parents in Vietnam, I always said nice things about America, that I was happy, because I didn't want my parents to worry about me. In the lunchroom, I sat alone on the first day. I ate American food for the first time. It tasted so different. I couldn't eat it. But I was hungry, so I swallowed hard. I ate and tears were running down my cheeks. I couldn't stop them.

Tung Anh Cao, Vietnamese

3

▲▲▲▲▲▲▲▲▲▲

Everybody misses their friends where ever they are when they move to another place. Close friends make people feel good. Everybody needs friends when they are alone. Sometimes people would like to know another person but they can't, because they are shy.

Having a friend is the most wonderful thing you can have because you can get help and you won't feel lonely.

Erika Meza-Duran

▲▲▲▲▲▲▲▲▲▲

This shell
reminds me of the refugee camp
on a single island in the Pacific Ocean
at whose beach I went swimming every day.
It reminds me of the peaceful and lovely days
on the beach in Vietnam with my mom and dad
before my dad died
and of the memories
between me and a boy I liked.
We swam and talked and ate together
everyday,
before he left me
about six months after
we'd gotten to know each other.
He gave me a shell.

Mimi Dam, Vietnamese

▲▲▲▲▲▲▲▲▲▲

In Laos we had 10 chickens, 10 pigs, 2 cows, 4 goats, 2 horses, and no money. We had a garden. It was planted with a lot of things. We went to the garden in the morning. It was planted with weeds, potatoes, corn, onions, cucumbers, and other vegetables. We worked all day.

The Communists were going to capture us and put us in jail…So my dad took us away at midnight. We walked in the woods about 45 days. There were 20 of us, my family and cousins. I was little, about 4 or 5 years old.

I was crying because I didn't have anything to eat or drink. And my cousin picked me up and carried me. We stopped for a rest. The guy that was holding me cut a branch off a tree and it had water in it. He drank it a little bit and let me drink the rest. I didn't cry anymore.

Then we came to the Mekong River. We cut something that looked like a boat. It was dark. We crossed the river in about 2 or 3 hours. When we got to the other side it was Thailand. Then they took us to the refugee camp. We were poor in the refugee camp, but they gave us rice and fish.

We left Laos and came to America because we are poor and there is too much war…We came to Thailand in 1983. We came to America in 1986.

When we first came to America, it seemed like a different world. Because I haven't ride a plane or car before. And here you don't have to walk like in Thailand or Laos. The streets are different and most things are different. Here they have computer and we don't in Laos, and people eat lunch here but we don't eat lunch there. We just eat rice for breakfast and dinner. Here they have coats, gloves, snow, glass, maps, lights, but in Laos we don't. The houses are different because our house there is made out of wood and here its made out of brick.

Moua Pao, Hmong

▲▲▲▲▲▲▲▲▲▲

In Jamaica
it was so warm and beautiful.
Sometimes we went to school
and sometimes we danced.

Jackie, Jamaican

▲▲▲▲▲▲▲▲▲▲

When I was young I moved to the country, and I lived with my mother, father, and my brother and sister. I always played basketball with my friends when I was living in Santo Domingo. I used to fight with my friends a lot when I went to school. We didn't fight when we went to the beach. We used to go fishing a lot, too. When I came home after playing or swimming, or fishing, my mother cooked rice and beef for me. My favorite game to play when I was a child was hide and seek. I never got caught.

Edgar Rivera, Dominican

▲▲▲▲▲▲▲▲▲▲

Everything is new to us. Things we dreamed have become real. Things we never saw, now we have seen; and what we never had, now we have. We seem to be like a baby that has just been born.

Tou Vang, Hmong

▲▲▲▲▲▲▲▲▲▲

When I was a little girl, I lived with my parents in Vietnam. My parents had two houses. One house was in the city of Saigon and one house was in the suburbs. When school opened I studied in Saigon. In the summer I lived in the suburbs. I had many friends, but I had just one best friend. She loved only me and I her. Her name is Huynh Loan, and we felt very happy. Usually we jumped rope and we swam in the swimming pool. We were afraid of lizards. My family always ate crayfish, fish, meat rolls and fried chicken. The time flitted away, we grew up, we were best friends through fifteen years. We have many memories of our childhood.

I loved my houses. I loved that place. I loved everything about my life. Then I came to the United States. I left my best friend, she felt heartbroken. She always has written letters to me. She tells about our youth. When I read the letters, I feel bitter sweet.

Anh Nguyet Nguyen, Vietnamese

Responding to Reading

Sharing Ideas

1. Share with your class some things about your life in your country. Talk about:
- ▲ where you lived,
- ▲ what your house was like,
- ▲ where you went to school,
- ▲ what you liked to do,
- ▲ who your friends were,
- ▲ what your favorite foods were.

2. Why did your family come to the United States? Talk about:
- ▲ how old you were,
- ▲ your trip from your country to this country,
- ▲ your life back home,
- ▲ why you left,
- ▲ friends or relatives you knew here.

3. What were your first impressions of the United States? Talk about:
- ▲ the food,
- ▲ the weather,
- ▲ the people,
- ▲ your new school,
- ▲ your new friends,
- ▲ shopping in the United States.

4. Sometimes, to get accepted in a new place, we do or say things that are not "us." Talk about a time you did or said something just to fit in with your new friends. What feelings did you experience during the incident?

5. Would you like to live in your country again? Why or why not? Talk about:
- ▲ what you miss, or don't miss,
- ▲ pleasant, or unpleasant, memories of home,

▲ things you like, or don't like, about the United States,

▲ things you like, or don't like, about life in your country.

6. What is your reaction to the student writings in this section? Talk about:

▲ feelings you have that are similar to these students',

▲ experiences you had that are similar to these students',

▲ why these young people came to the United States,

▲ what problems they had,

▲ their emotional reactions to the United States,

▲ your favorite readings.

7. How many different cultures are represented in these readings? Did they have similar or different experiences from each other?

8. Have a culture day in your class. Introduce the other students in your class to your culture. Bring in clothing, food, pictures, music, games, and books. Give a little history of your country. Have someone list the things that are different or similar in the cultures in your class.

Writing About Our Old and New Lives

1. Write about your life before you came to the United States. Write about:

▲ your family,

▲ your school,

▲ your house,

▲ your friends,

▲ your pets,

▲ your food.

2. Was life in your country similar or different from the students in this section?

3. Write about your trip from your country to the United States. Write about:

▲ your preparation to leave,

▲ what you left behind, and what you took,

▲ the day you left, and what feelings you had,

▲ how you got to this country, how long it took, what city you first came to, who was there to greet you, your feelings when you arrived.

4. Write about your adjustment to life in the United States. What was difficult? easy? different? new? exciting? dangerous? Who in your family had the hardest, or easiest, time adjusting to their new life?

5. Imagine you can write a letter to one of the students in this section. Which student will you select? Why? What do you want to tell them? Write the letter and share it with your class.

6. Imagine your brother or sister is still waiting to come to the United States. Write a letter of advice to your brother or sister.

7. Does your culture make it easier, or harder, for you to adjust to life in the United States? Is part of your culture in conflict with life in the United States? Do you ever feel caught in the middle? Which culture do you prefer?

More Reading

My Home in Mexico, Donna Bailey. Steck-Vaughn, 1990.

Boat People, Tana Reiff. Fearon/Janus/Quercus, 1989.

My Home in Russia, Jenny Vaughan. Steck-Vaughn, 1990.

Family Pictures, Cuadros de Familia, Carmen Garza Lomas. Children's Press, 1990.

New Kids On The Block: Oral Histories of Immigrant Teens, Janet Bode. Franklin Watts, 1989.

Lee Ann, the Story of a Vietnamese Girl, Tricia Brown. G. P. Putnam's Sons, 1971.

Dan Thuy's New Life in America, Karen O'Conner. Lerner Publications, 1992.

Portraits of Mexican Americans, Dr. Theresa Perez. Good Apple Press, 1991.

A Visit in the Philippines, Donna Bailey and Anna Sproule. Steck-Vaughn, 1991.

The Puerto Ricans in America, Ronald J. Larsen. Lerner Publications Company, 1989.

Tales from Gold Mountain: Stories of the Chinese in the New World, Paul Yee. Macmillan, 1990.

A Long Way From Home, Maureen Crane Wartski. Westminster John Knox, 1980.

In the Year of the Boar and Jackie Robinson, Bette Bao Lord. Harper and Row, 1984.

Tales of Love

Love and joy are twins. They are born of each other.

William Hazlitt

The Love Stone

Life in a refugee camp is hard. In this story, love made it easier. But when one person left for the United States and the other person stayed behind, would their love survive the separation?

Part 1

One day in the refugee camp, I met a boy my own age. Each day we shared our dreams.

"I want to be a teacher," I said. "They help children have a better life."

"I want to be an artist," he said. "Everywhere I look I see a picture. I want to paint my life and my struggle for freedom."

Each day I helped in the school, and each day he drew pictures. He had a sketchbook he called "Camp Life" and it was full of his drawings. He drew the palm trees, the hills, the children, the houses, the trucks, the people coming and going, the teachers, the hospital.

Sometimes he drew just the two of us. Under each picture he wrote the words: "Where there is love, there is joy." Yes, even in a refugee camp he brought me joy and I brought him joy. I only needed to see his smiling face to feel good. I only needed to hear his happy voice. The long days seemed shorter then. The long wait to go to the United States and our new life seemed possible.

We were together every day. But then one day I heard these words over the loudspeaker: "Those people whose names are on the U.S.A. resettlement list, please come to the delegation's office to receive your passports."

His name was on the list. My name wasn't. Now we would part.

VOCABULARY

shared talked about
sketchbook book for drawing pictures
precious possession most important thing you own
stung hurt

Tears ran down my cheeks. He was crying, too. He touched my hand for the last time.

"Take my drawings," he said, handing me his book, his most precious possession. "Keep them until we meet again."

"No," I said. "Bring your drawings to the United States. Show them to people so they will know about our struggle for freedom. Tell them not to forget us here."

"Then take this," he said, and he put a beautiful stone into my shaking hand. "I will wait for you in the United States."

The bus came and he left. The dust from the wheels stung my eyes. I waved and he waved back through the open window. Then he was gone.

Part 2

The next day, the refugee camp seemed dirty through my salty tears. Everywhere I looked now I saw people crying. I saw people sick. I saw people with no hope, people with war wounds, people with dead relatives, people who were too old or too sick to go to a new country.

How can the camp change like this? No, I thought, it is I who have changed because he is gone. Now I knew in my heart the meaning of his words: "Where there is love, there is joy." For us there had been joy even among misery and despair because there had been love.

VOCABULARY

misery suffering
despair   no hope
trembling   shaking

Then I remembered the stone, the love stone, that he had given me. I took it out of my pocket with trembling hands and tied it around my neck, like a necklace. I did it quickly, like a thirsty person suddenly finding water. I felt the cool stone against my skin and I felt better. Then I thought of him.

Where is he now? Will I see him again? Does he still love me? Will our love survive this separation?

For weeks and weeks the love stone was all I had. I helped in the school. I did all the same things, but it was just my body now, not my mind. My mind was someplace else, sick from loneliness, wondering now how I would survive the refugee camp. Would I ever really go to the United States? Would I die here, never seeing freedom and him again?

Then one day someone handed me a letter. It was the American teacher who helped us with our English. She was crying.

"Here is a letter for you," she said. "It is from the United States." Her tears were tears of joy.

I knew the handwriting on the outside of the letter and I opened it quickly. He was in the United States with his family. He described his new life, the food, the people, the cars, and the freedom, and I knew he was happy. In the letter there was a drawing. It was a small drawing that just fit in the tiny envelope. It was a picture of the two of us. Under the picture were the words: "Where there is love, there is joy. I will wait for you forever."

Part 3

Something hot ran down my cheek. It was my tears again. They fell on the letter and I wrote him back. For months and months I waited. Then our names were called. We received our passports and I looked at the refugee camp for the last time. Good-bye, I thought, looking at the palm trees and the school and the dusty roads. How can I love you like this when I've been waiting so long to leave you? Now it was my turn to wave through the open window of the bus to all the people still waiting and waiting in the dust for their names to be called.

We flew to San Francisco. Our long struggle for freedom was over. The plane landed and we walked through the crowd at the airport. Would he be there? I had written him. But where was his town? Maybe he lived too far away. Maybe he didn't get my letter.

I looked and looked and then I saw him. He was standing with his parents, so shy, so beautiful, seeing only me among all the faces at the airport. Even from a distance, I could see his eyes were full of tears.

"Here," he said after we had met and talked. He handed me a new drawing. The drawing showed a lonely boy reaching his arm out toward an empty page. The picture was only half-done.

"Now," he said, "I can finish my picture." He quickly drew my face and under the picture he wrote the words: "Where there is love, there is joy."

Who Can Say What Love Is?

Who can say what love is?
Love is clear like water,
And high as the sky.
Love for your Motherland is forever,
Love for your people never fades.

Who can say what love is?
We love our dad, mom, grandma and grandpa,
Those who gave us birth,
And raised us to become a man or woman.
And taught us to respect our teachers,
Those who helped us cross the river.
No matter if the river was shallow or deep,
They tried to push the boat for us.

To be a good person, be modest,
Respect older people.
The words of parents and teachers
Are deep like the ocean and high as clouds.

Trang Nguyen, Vietnamese

Hush, My Darling

Has anyone ever laughed at your name? In this story, a small girl from Lebanon is laughed at by the other children. They think her name is funny because it is different. The child is hurt.

The school bus stopped on the streets of Dearborn, Michigan. Hoda Chamy got out. The wind blew her long black hair. The wind blew her schoolbag. The wind blew her soft face, but it did not blow her tears away.

"*Ma baluki?* What's wrong, child?" her mother asked, opening the door. "*Limatha tabkeen?* Why are you crying?"

Hoda didn't answer.

"*Ayna jadatuki?* Where is Grandma?" she finally sobbed.

"*Nayma.* Sleeping," her mother said.

Hoda opened the bedroom door, the only bedroom for six people. Grandma was sitting by the window. Hoda ran to her, crying and crying. Grandma stroked her forehead and held her.

"*Indaee ya habeebatee.* Hush, my darling," Grandma whispered, wiping her tears and holding her...holding her...holding her...as she had done since birth. "My beautiful Hoda. *Indaee ya habeebatee.* Hush, my darling."

Hoda wanted to hear those words. They brought her peace and comfort whenever she was hurt.

"Tell me again, Grandma," Hoda sobbed, burying her face in her grandma's lap. "Tell me about my name."

"Your name?" Grandma said.

"Yes, my name. Tell me what it means again."

"It means 'gift,'" Grandma said kindly.

"Tell me the rest. Please, Grandma. Tell me the rest."

"It means 'gift,'" Grandma continued, "and that's what you are, a beautiful gift, kind and soft and gentle. To me, to your mother, to your father, to your friends, to your relatives, you are a gift. Why do you ask?"

"Because today they laughed, the other kids laughed at my name and it hurts."

Grandma held her tighter. Grandma stroked her forehead. Grandma wiped her tears.

"It hurts, Grandma, all over."

Grandma whispered the words again. "*Indaee ya habeebatee, Hoda.* Hush, my darling," she said softly, like a cool breeze, holding the small child to her chest, "My beautiful Hoda. *Indaee ya habeebatee.* Hush, my darling."

"Why do they do it?" Hoda sobbed. "Don't they know that is all I have? *Indee isin. Hatha kul ma indee.* I have a name and nothing more. I don't have blue eyes. I don't have money. I don't have a big house. I don't speak English. All I have is a name, and when they laugh at my name, they laugh at me, at all that I am. And it hurts. And I want to go away. I want to go home, away from here, far, far away."

"Hush, my darling," Grandma whispered, her own eyes clouding with tears now. "Hush, hush, my beautiful one. It doesn't matter what others think or say. *Ma muhim ma bikulu naas aw shu bee fakru.* Your name means 'gift,' and to us you will always be a beautiful gift."

Forever is a Long Time

Rosita and Manuel loved each other. They spent a day together exploring San Francisco. The sights and sounds of the city were wonderful. Surely something as beautiful as their love would last forever. Or would it? Someone in their life was not so sure.

Part 1

Rosita and Manuel stood together waiting for a cable car on a San Francisco street. Manuel touched her hand.

"Come on," Manuel whispered. "Let's catch this one."

Together they ran for the cable car. Their feet were light on the summer street. They laughed and jumped on the moving car. They had the whole day to explore San Francisco, and their love made it special.

VOCABULARY

San Francisco   a city in California
let's catch this one   let's ride this one
Tacoma   a city in Washington State
lever   the brake handle

"Eight people to a side, please!" the conductor called. "Eight people! You people in the doorway, either move inside or get off the car, please! There will be another car in three minutes!"

Rosita put her head on Manuel's shoulder. They whispered to each other while the car rolled along the San Francisco street. The cable car was full of tourists and Manuel and Rosita listened to their voices.

"I can't believe it's this cold anywhere in August, Dolores. If I ever come back here I'm bringing my winter coat."

"They used to have these cars in Tacoma, Al."

"George, what should we get Darlene? I have gifts for everyone but her."

Then the cable car went up a huge hill. At the top of the hill the tourists snapped pictures of the bay in the fog far below.

"Have you ever seen anything so beautiful, Rose?"

"Going down!" the conductor called. "Hang on, please!" The conductor pulled back on a long lever. The cable car jerked and slowed down and Rosita held on to Manuel's arm. She could smell the burning cable oil as the car started down the hill. She caught her breath and looked down the steep street.

Part 2

The cable car ride ended near Fisherman's Wharf. Manuel took Rosita's hand and they jumped off the car. They walked past the Maritime Museum and Ghirardelli Square. Artists were painting on the street corners and musicians were playing music. Sea gulls sat on posts near the fishing boats. In the distance the red span of the Golden Gate Bridge disappeared into puffs of white clouds.

VOCABULARY

Alcatraz   a famous prison in the United States
pier   long dock
intersection   where two streets cross

Rosita and Manuel walked hand-in-hand past the open air gift shops on the wharf. Tourists were everywhere buying cable car ashtrays, giant sand dollars, porcupine fish from Mexico, conch shells from the Caribbean, mushroom coral, tiny sea horses from the Indian Ocean, dolls made of seashells and, of course, pictures and postcards of San Francisco.

"Look at this postcard," Manuel said, laughing. "Alcatraz— Having a wonderful time! Wish you were here!"

They walked out on the People's Pier. The pier curved like a banana far out into the bay. They sat for a moment on a concrete bench and rested.

"The sailboats are beautiful," Rosita said.

"There's Treasure Island," Manuel said, "and the Bay Bridge."

People all along the pier were fishing. They kept their fish in buckets filled with water. Some people had crab nets and they were catching dozens of crabs. Little children laughed and chased the sea gulls.

"I can see why nobody escaped from Alcatraz," Manuel said. They both laughed. The prison sat on a rock far out in the middle of the bay. Rosita rested her head on Manuel's shoulder and they sat quietly in the sun.

When they were hungry they walked back to the wharf and ate together. Then they walked to the corner of Hyde and Beach and waited for a cable car again. There were white lines all over the intersection and two sets of tracks. One set was for the cars full of people going back up Hyde Street and the other set was for the empty cars which had to be turned around.

"Don't get on the cable car until it has been completely turned around!" the conductor called. "Wait until it is off the turntable, please!"

"Gregory! Daniel!" a man called. "Take your mother to the side of the cable car so I can get your picture."

"All aboard!" the conductor said.

Manuel and Rosita held on again. The first block was a small hill. The second block was steep.

"Going up!" the conductor yelled. "Hang on, please!" He pulled back on a long lever. The cable car jerked forward and began the slow beautiful climb up the steep street.

Manuel and Rosita watched the city go by again. The city sounds were happy sounds because they were happy. Their thoughts were on each other and they were beautiful thoughts.

Part 3

Toward the end of the afternoon, Manuel and Rosita rode a bus to Golden Gate Park and sat on a hillside together under a huge eucalyptus tree. A long meadow stretched green and fragrant beneath them. Overhead sea gulls floated in the sky. Young people with packs on their backs, some carrying guitars, walked by. Old people stood in groups and talked about past times. Cars honked on Stanyon Street. Families peddled rented bikes down green paths. Chinese children with black hair and round faces ran by, laughing and playing. Dogs chased Frisbees and squirrels. There were flute players and jugglers. The breeze blew through the eucalyptus tree and the scent was wonderful.

VOCABULARY

fragrant smelling nice
rented borrowed
scent smell
para siempre "forever" in Spanish
quivering moving in the wind

Manuel looked into Rosita's eyes and they were beautiful. Rosita looked into Manuel's eyes and they were beautiful. Then their lips touched under the blue sky.

"*Para siempre.* Forever," Manuel whispered.

"*Para siempre.* Forever," Rosita whispered back.

The huge eucalyptus tree smiled at the two lovers. Forever? the old tree whispered to the gulls. Forever? the old tree whispered to the afternoon breeze. Forever? the old tree whispered to the quivering grass on the hillside.

Maybe.

The Flower Cloth

In this story, an old Hmong woman wants to finish some-thing. She lives in a refugee camp in Thailand. Her needle-work is called paj ntaub *(pon dow) by the Hmong people. It means "flower cloth" and it is beautiful. Life in the refugee camp was not easy for the Hmong people, but to return to their country of Laos meant death. The Hmong people were determined, however, to start life over.*

"Rau-siab rau yam twg yeej yuav tau yam ntawd,"
they said.

"Put your heart into something and you will succeed and get that thing."

The old Hmong woman sat on the stone without speaking. The noise of the refugee camp filled the air, but she didn't hear it. She grabbed the string on the loom and started her day's work. She was weaving a tapestry, a *paj ntaub*. In the flower cloth was the story of her life.

She worked quickly. Her body was old, but her fingers were determined. Her fingers moved by themselves, weaving the sorrow of her life into the beautiful cloth. First she stitched the border, the blue and white triangles that symbolized the hills of Laos, her home. Then she stitched her life as a child. She was happy. She was with her family. They had chickens and pigs and rice. There was peace in the village.

Then she stitched her life as a young woman. She wore silver and she was beautiful. Her bride price was high and she had healthy children. They planted and harvested rice together and lived their life according to the Hmong year.

VOCABULARY

refugee camp   where people go to escape war
loom   a machine used to make a cloth
weave   to sew
tapestry   a beautiful cloth
border   outer edge
bride price   money paid to parents for a wife
helicopter   a type of airplane
mist from the air   poison gas

In the middle of the tapestry, however, there were helicopters and people crying. War started and the men in the village were killed. Mist from the air burned their skin. Many people died and were left behind. Others ran through the forest, eating jungle plants and hiding during the day. Everyone was afraid. Finally, they floated across the Mekong River at night and waited in the refugee camp.

She wove all of this into the flower cloth, thread by thread, color by color, in beautiful blue and white, all the sorrow of her life. Life as she knew it was gone forever, and she wanted to stitch its memory into the cloth, so the children and grandchildren of the Hmong people would know their history.

Then one day a small child came to her.

"Grandma," the child said. "The bus is here."

The old woman said nothing. She kept weaving her cloth. She didn't even look up.

"Please, Grandma, please," the child said. "We're going to the United States. Won't you change your mind?"

The old woman looked into the pleading eyes of the child. This was her favorite grandson. She had cared for him as a baby. When he had cried as a small boy, she had comforted him. Then she had carried him on her back through the jungle to freedom, across the river and into the camp.

"*Lawv xa koj los xwb, los sab?*" she asked. "The others sent you, didn't they?"

"Yes."

"*Nws tsis pab tau dab tsi li.* It won't do any good," she said, trying to sound gruff. "*Kuv yuav tsum ua kom tag daim paj ntaub.* I must finish the flower cloth. *Muaj ib hnub twg koj mam li to taub.* Someday you will understand. *Mus, cov me nyuam nej sawv daws mus.* Go, child. *Nyob ntawm no nws yuav tsis muaj dabtsi zoo rau nej, tsuas yog txoj kev tuag xwb.* There is nothing for you here but death."

One by one her family came to say good-bye to her. Three daughters. There were no sons left. Twelve grandchildren. There were no husbands left. They cried and kissed her. They brought her flowers and food. They put flowers in her lap and begged, but still her fingers kept working.

"*Kuv yuav tsum ua kom tag daim paj ntaub.* I must finish the flower cloth. Then I can die. I'm sorry. *Mus ceeb tam simno.* Go, quickly, please. *Kuv laus heev lawm kuv tsis mus.* I'm too old to go."

The crowded bus left the camp. People who were not on the bus cried and waved.

"Maybe the next bus will be yours!" someone yelled, waving to a relative for the last time. "We will meet in America! There is food and work! We can become people again!"

The small child looked back through the dust on the road. His grandmother sat alone on the rock. Her head, old and tired, was on her chest. Her body was tiny, like a bird, but her fingers were moving, determined to finish what she had started. They worked by themselves, weaving the sorrow of her life into the flower cloth.

"Good-bye, Grandma," he whispered, through the choking dust and noise, through the shouts of joy and tears of separation. "I will always love you."

Please Don't Leave (Txhob Ncaim)

A Hmong love song

Even though I smile on the outside,
Inside my heart I cry, please don't leave.
I want us to stay together forever,
Like the sun and the moon.
My heart is rushing and broken,
Like a wild river,
My heart, my feelings, are like the moving clouds,
Always changing, with no place to rest.
My Beloved, is there any day, or any way,
That we will meet again?
Will our separation be for days?
Or will it be for months?
Please, let us meet again before we die.
Wherever you go,
I hope you have a happy life,
Free of sorrow.
No matter what happens,
I will miss you forever.

Mr. Lue Lee

Responding to Reading

Sharing Ideas

1. Each story in this section describes different forms of love. For example, "The Flower Cloth" is about an old woman who loves her culture and is sad when it is destroyed. It is also about a small boy who loves his grandmother.

- ▲ What other forms of love do you see in these stories?
- ▲ What is love?
- ▲ Is love between two people "forever?"

2. Find stories of love in the newspaper or magazines. Share them with your class. Is love common to every culture?

3. In the story "The Love Stone," the two main characters come to the United States. What problems do immigrants have when they come to a new country?

4. Act out one of the stories in this section. Ask your teacher to arrange a performance for another class.

5. Make a flower cloth, a *paj ntaub,* of your own life. Use paper and colors. What will you draw? What colors will you use? Hang your flower cloth where others can see it.

Writing About Love

1. Complete the following sentences:

- ▲ Love is…
- ▲ One thing I love to do is…
- ▲ I once loved a person named…
- ▲ Twenty things I love are…

2. Do you have a favorite love song, poem, or phrase? Write it down and share it with the class.

3. Write about love for your homeland. Who did you leave behind? What was your life like? Who were your friends? What do you miss?

4. List ten words from the story "Forever Is A Long Time" which describe San Francisco.

5. Write a love poem. An easy way to start is to think about the five senses:
- ▲ Love tastes like…
- ▲ Love smells like…
- ▲ Love sounds like…
- ▲ Love feels like…
- ▲ Love looks like…

6. In "The Flower Cloth," the woman was determined to do something. Write about a time you were determined to do something. Did you succeed?

More Reading

The Giving Tree, Shel Silverstein. Harper and Row, 1964, 1988.

I Speak English For My Mom, Muriel Stanck. A. Whitman, 1989.

My Best Friend, Mee-Yung Kim, Dianne MacMillan and Dorothy Freeman. Julian Messner Press, 1989.

The Most Beautiful Place In The World, Ann Cameron. Alfred A. Knopf, 1988.

The Gift, Helen Coutant. Alfred A. Knopf, 1983.

My Best Friend Tony Santos, Phyllis S. Yingling. Julian Messner Publishing, 1988.

Sarah, Plain and Tall, Patricia MacLachlan. Harper and Row, 1985.

Annie and the Old One, Miska Miles. Little, Brown, 1971.

Squanto and the First Thanksgiving, Joyce Kessel. Carolrhoda Books, 1983.

A Couple of Kooks: And Other Stories About Love, Cynthia Rylant. Orchard Books, 1990.

Gilberto and the Wind, Marie Hall Ets. Viking Press, 1963.

Hello, Amigos! Tricia Brown. Holt, Rinehart and Winston, 1986.

All In A Day, Mitsumasa Anno and Raymond Briggs. Philomel Books, 1986.

Molly's Pilgrim, Barbara Cohen. Lothrop, Lee, and Shepard Books, 1983.

Tales of Courage

You must do the thing you think you cannot do.

Eleanor Roosevelt

In December and Afterwards

The Story of Vika Ivchenko

Ukraine is now a free country. For many years it was part of the former Soviet Union. Life in Ukraine was difficult then, and many Ukrainian people came to live in the United States. In this true story of love and courage, they bring a young Ukrainian girl, a gifted poet, to the United States to try to save her life after the nuclear disaster at Chernobyl.

Part 1

Beautiful Victoria (Vika) Ivchenko was born in Kiev, the capital of Ukraine, in 1980. She loved poetry. Even before she could read and write, she told her poems to her mother and her mother wrote them down.

VOCABULARY

nuclear power plant   produces electricity
Chernobyl   a city in Ukraine
invisible   can not be seen
radiation   harmful invisible energy
fatigue   exhaustion

"What a beautiful poem, Vika," Halyna Ivchenko said, taking a pencil and paper and writing down tiny Vika's words. They were happy poems. They were about her grandfather and animals and toys.

But early one morning there was an explosion in the nuclear power plant in Chernobyl, 37 miles away. It was April 26, 1986. Vika was asleep. The next day when she was outside riding her bike, a huge invisible cloud of radiation blew over Kiev. Within hours her exposed skin turned bright red. She developed a fever, extreme fatigue, and severe vomiting.

"What is wrong, Vika?" her mother asked. There was no news on the television about the explosion. The doctor told them not to worry.

Ukrainian people in Kiev, however, said there had been an explosion at Chernobyl, that huge amounts of radiation escaped into the air. Soon trucks full of burned people came to the Kiev hospital from Chernobyl. But still there was no official news about the disaster.

Part 2

Vika became terribly sick. Her immune system was damaged from the radiation. Her friends were sick, too. All of them drank water and milk poisoned with radiation. Vika struggled to get well, but the medical help for her was poor.

Vika was six now and learning to read and write. Now she could write down her own poems, but her poems changed. Ukrainian people were dying from the Chernobyl disaster. Many of them were her friends. Her poems were no longer those of a small and happy child.

VOCABULARY

immune system   protects the body from illness
damaged   hurt
extinguish   put out

"Before Chernobyl her poems were happy," her mother said, "but after Chernobyl they became serious and philosophical."

In this poem, written when Vika was ten, she describes her feelings on the fifth anniversary of the Chernobyl disaster:

The Sentence

Ukraine, oh, my Ukraine,
Unhappy mother of mine,
I am your child of misfortune,
Who is lost in faraway places,
Tell me, how can we save you?
How can we extinguish the pain of Chernobyl?
You greet me like a mother,
But without the bread and salt.*
Your salt is bitter from strontium and iodine
And your bread does not give life anymore.
Your children are sick from radiation,
Like camera film ruined by the light.
Your radiated children have flown away
To look for a better life.

*(*It is a custom in Ukraine to greet visitors in your house with bread and salt.)*

31

"And sometimes she was just a little girl again," her mother said, "writing about things in her childhood." In this poem, written when Vika was seven, she describes walking to school on a foggy morning:

The Fog

This morning autumn was carrying milk.
She tried hard not to spill it.
But then she slipped and fell,
And now the morning air is foggy.
The sky is holding houses on its hands
And the trees are blowing in the clouds.
I run scared to school.
What if I should suddenly get lost in the fog?

By the time Vika was only seven, children all over Ukraine were reading her poems. She was on the radio and television. When she was nine, she published her first book of poetry. The book contains 45 poems. She named the book *In December and Afterwards* because she was born in the month of December.

When Vika was ten, she published her second book of poems. This book contained 70 poems. She named the book *And I'm Growing Like the Grass Through Asphalt.* The title means that she is trying to grow despite her difficult childhood (Chernobyl, the divorce of her mother and father, and the struggle of Ukrainian people for independence from Russia).

Part 3

Many people loved Vika for her poetry now. She appeared on Moscow television. She received an important scholarship from the Soviet government. She was the only Ukrainian child to receive the award.

But Vika's health was poor. Doctors in Moscow did not want to treat Chernobyl victims. In May, 1991, the lymph nodes swelled in her neck. Sores developed on her legs. She had repeated respiratory infections. She was weak and lost weight. Halyna Ivchenko was afraid that her beautiful daughter was dying.

The Ukrainian people in Minnesota, however, found out about Vika. They read her poems and wanted to save her life. They sponsored Vika and Halyna through a church in Minnesota.

"We are going to the United States, Vika," her mother said one day. She was very happy. "There are many Ukrainian people who love us there and you will receive good medical care."

In March, 1992, Vika and Halyna Ivchenko came to Minnesota. Children's Hospital in St. Paul agreed to give Vika free medical care and she entered the hospital immediately after arriving in the United States. At first the doctors thought she needed a bone marrow transplant. Then they decided that wasn't necessary. Now they are trying to strengthen her immune system with medicine.

Slowly, Vika is getting better. She loves American fast food, and she tasted pizza for the first time. Her first impression of the United States was "All Americans smile, even to strangers."

Vika was surprised at the number of Ukrainian people in the United States and how they have preserved Ukrainian culture. "I see more Ukrainian culture here than I did back home. The Ukrainian people here preserve our art, like Easter egg decorating and embroidery."

"And Americans love their country," Vika says. "They love to preserve beauty for the future and their children."

In addition to being a poet, Vika Ivchenko also sings, plays the piano and the guitar, paints, speaks three languages, is an excellent knitter, and loves to bake with her mother.

According to Halyna, Vika had another experience which affected her life.

"One day after Chernobyl, Vika had a religious experience," her mother said. "She asked to be baptized in church one day. She said she needed it. So she was baptized in the Orthodox Church."

Later Vika wrote this poem. She was nine. It was four years after the disaster at Chernobyl.

The Prayer

I am praying to God for one thing,
To protect the people that I love so much.
May they never be unhappy.
May their faces never age.
And may I go to a far away country,
So I can forget these sorrows,
And remember only the good things.
This is my precious dream.
But if I do not see these people again,
How can I return goodness to them a hundred times over?
Protect, O God, these people who I love.

The Video Arcade

Sok Chunn was tired of war. He was glad when his family escaped from Cambodia and came to the United States. But the memories of war did not go away for him. In this story, he struggles with those memories.

Part 1

Sok Chunn got in the car with his American friends. Pete drove. He had a nice car. They turned the radio on and drove to the mall. On the way they talked and laughed.

When they got to the mall they went to the game room. It was full of American kids all dressed alike. They wore blue jeans cut open at the knees, expensive gym shoes, and colored T-shirts. Everyone was crowded around machines that lit up and made beeping noises.

Sok exchanged his money for game tokens. Then he sat down in the low seat of a race car. He put a token in the slot and the screen lit up. He pushed the pedal on the floor and started the race. Smash! His car hit another car and he laughed. He pushed the pedal again and skidded around the track.

Next he sat in a helicopter cockpit. The screen lit up with soldiers and tanks and airplanes trying to shoot him down. He aimed his guns and fired. Bullets from his guns smashed into the soldiers on the screen and his score lit up. He was a good shot.

But something didn't feel right about the video games today and Sok was glad when the game was over. He found Pete and they played air hockey for a while. Then Pete wanted to play another army game.

"Here comes a tank!" Pete hollered. "BAM! BAM! BAM! Did you see that? Look out on the left! Come on, shoot your gun! BAM! BAM! BAM!" Airplanes, tanks, and soldiers broke into pieces on the screen.

Sok tried to play but couldn't. There was sweat on the back of his neck. Fear swirled around his face and stuck in his stomach. Pictures from the past flashed across the inside of his forehead like a movie. They were pictures of war and he didn't want to see them, but he couldn't shut the pictures out because they were inside his head.

Part 2

Sok shook his head, but the pictures of war were still there. He knew what they were. Not long ago there were real soldiers in his life. There were real helicopters. There were real bullets. The dead were real. The blood was real. The screams were real. None of this was fun for him today.

Last night he had had the same dream again, too. He knew the dream was making him uncomfortable today. Whenever he had that dream it took him two or three days to forget it. The dream was always the same. The Khmer Rouge soldiers were emptying Phnom Penh. He was walking out of the city with his family. The Khmer Rouge soldiers were just boys his own age and they were Cambodian just like him. They wore red headbands and they were heroes because they had freed the capital city. But then they started killing people and the walk turned into terror.

In his nightmare the Khmer Rouge soldiers were trying to kill him and his gun wouldn't work right. The soldiers came closer and closer but he couldn't get his gun to work. When he finally pulled the trigger, no bullets came out. He tried to run away but his feet were heavy with mud. He tried to climb a hill, but there was sand on the hill and he kept sliding back down, and the soldiers kept getting closer.

Finally he made it to the top of the hill, but his gun jammed again and his grenades didn't explode. Then the Khmer Rouge soldiers made a circle around him and stared at him with frightful faces. He always woke up sweating.

"Pete," he said, "I'm sorry, but I need to walk awhile. I'll meet you later, okay? How about two o'clock?"

"Are you all right?" Pete asked.

"Yeah, I'm all right," Sok answered. "I just need to walk a bit."

Pete put his hand on Sok's shoulder. Pete knew him well and cared about him. He understood Cambodia and what happened there. They had watched *The Killing Fields* together.

"Did you have that dream again?" Pete asked.

"Yeah. Last night. It takes me a while the next day. These games are getting to me, and all this noise. I'm sorry. Two o'clock?"

"Two o'clock," Pete said. "Do you want some company?"

"No, that's all right."

Part 3

Sok left the game room and walked around the mall. The mall was beautiful. There was nothing like this in Cambodia. The mall had flowers and small trees growing under sunny skylights. People were shopping and playing with their children. Everyone was happy. The stores were full of clothes and gifts. There were wonderful places to eat. Everything was bright and colorful.

Sok sat in a new car that a company was giving away. He put his name and address on a slip of paper and pushed it into a box. Then he heard music and he stopped to listen. Musicians were playing live music on a stage. The music was cheerful and people were singing. The man next to Sok had his small son on his shoulders. The little boy was laughing and singing.

Sok felt better. He felt a lot better. He bought a cookie, fresh baked, and ate it. Then he went into a record store and listened to music. In the small listening room he put on a headset and listened to his favorite group. The music was close to his ears and helped him forget Cambodia. He still couldn't understand how Cambodians could kill Cambodians. How could anybody hate that much? "Aw, forget it," he said to himself, and he turned the music up.

At two o'clock he met Pete and the others. They all went and had a pizza together. Then they left.

Part 4

Pete drove the other boys home. Then he drove Sok home.

"I have a present for your mother," Pete said to Sok. "It's something I bought for her at the mall. Do you mind if I come in for a minute?"

"No, that's fine," Sok said.

The boys walked in the house. Sok's mom was in the kitchen cooking rice and singing softly to herself. They were poor, but the house was clean and quiet. There was order and peace in their home. Sok needed it. His short life had been filled with war and chaos and now there was finally rest.

Pete took a fresh flower out of a bag and gave it to Sok's mother. She smiled graciously and bowed and said, "Thank you."

"Every time I see your mom I want to give her something," Pete said. "I see the pictures on the wall of your father and your brothers and sisters who died in Cambodia and I want to do something for her. I know nothing can bring her husband back, or her children, but I'm glad she's here and I'm glad you're here. You have friends in the United States."

Sok translated Pete's message. He spoke softly to his mother. His voice was full of love. His mother listened quietly to every word. There was pain on her face as she listened. There was pain in her eyes. Pete's words had opened up the past.

"Thank you," she whispered and Pete could see that her pain was deep. Her tiny body seemed weak and frail against the memories that would not go away.

But then she spoke again. Her voice was strong and full of courage. Her words came from her soul, not from her tired body.

"This is a good country," she said. "Here we start over. Many of our people did not make it here. They are dead, all gone. But we must begin again and think only about tomorrow."

She handed Pete a small package of rice.

"You're too thin," she said. "Eat."

The rice was still warm, like her heart, and she patted Pete on the shoulder like a mother.

"Sok still has dreams," she said. "Help him forget. Here we start over. Here we think only about tomorrow."

When Two Cultures Collide
The Story of Black Elk

Long ago, two different cultures met on the Great Plains of the United States. Only one survived. In this true story of courage, a Lakota medicine man serves his people as a healer. Years later, just before he dies, he tells his story to a white man in a famous book.

Black Elk was a Lakota Indian of the Ogalala band. He was born in 1863 on the Little Powder River in the month of December (the Month of the Popping Trees). His family lived in the Black Hills and his early childhood was happy. He described the Black Hills then as "a great mother which gave us food and everything we needed."

VOCABULARY

band group of people
vision like a dream
massacred killed

When Black Elk was nine, he had a great vision. In his vision he met six grandfathers who taught him many things about life. They also gave him the power to heal. He was carried in his vision to the top of Harney Peak in the Black Hills where he saw the whole world. In the middle of the world he saw a holy tree full of flowers and he knew that all people must live together in peace. When he awoke, he had been unconscious for 12 days.

The United States was expanding westward. War broke out between the United States and Native American tribes. The war ended in 1868 with a treaty which said the Black Hills belonged to the Lakota people forever. However, gold was discovered in the Black Hills and the war started again. This war continued until United States soldiers massacred 153 Lakota people at Wounded Knee Creek in South Dakota. It was December 29, 1890. On that day, the war between the Native American people and the expanding United States ended.

Despite being shot in the stomach, Black Elk survived this long war. He became a medicine man and healed many sick and wounded people. He was an inspiration to his people during this time of great suffering and loss.

In 1931 a white man named John Neihardt visited Black Elk. Black Elk was living on a reservation and was very old. He spoke no English, but he trusted John Neihardt. He agreed to tell John Neihardt the story of his life, including the details of his great vision which he had kept secret. This book, *Black Elk Speaks,* describes Lakota culture and gives a look at United States history through the eyes of a Lakota Indian.

The Boy Who Couldn't Speak

The Hmong people are from Laos. Their name means "free people." They fought with the United States against North Vietnam in the Vietnam War and rescued many American pilots. But thousands of Hmong people were killed when the Vietnam War ended. To escape death they walked through the jungle, swam the Mekong River, and lived in refugee camps in Thailand. Then most of them came to the United States. In this story, a Hmong boy struggles with his new life in the United States.

Part 1

Lee Vang hated school. Whenever he spoke his tongue didn't work right and all the other kids laughed.

"Hey, LLLLLLLee," they said. "HHHHHHow are yyyyyyou?"

Lee's tongue stopped working in Laos, the night his family tried to escape. He never told the kids in school how it happened, because whenever he talked, they laughed. So he finally stopped talking.

His tongue stopped working on the Mekong River. That was where the soldiers caught his family. His family had walked for days, hiding in the forest. Then they were caught at the river, just when they could see Thailand and safety.

VOCABULARY

Laos   a country in Southeast Asia

Mekong River   a river that divides Laos from Thailand

raft   a home-made boat made of floating wood

bamboo   a tree in south Asia

clan   the Hmong extended family unit

"Nyob zoo! Hide!"

Lee could still hear his father's voice.

"Ceev ceev! Ntawm cov nyoj! Quickly! In the tall grass!"

The soldiers shot his mother three times and she died. Then they threw his baby sister into the river. They found his father next. They took all his money, the money they had saved to pay the boatman to take them across the river to Thailand. Then they shot him and left. But they never found Lee. Lee was too quick. He hid in the tall grass until they were gone.

Lee's father didn't die right away. Lee found him bleeding to death in the grass.

"Here," his father said. "Take my knife. Make a raft out of bamboo the way I showed you. Float to the other side and find our clan in the camp. Go to America with them and start a new life. *Nyob ntawm no tsis muaj dabtsi zoo rau koj lawm tsuas yog txog kev tuag xwb.* There's nothing for you here but death."

Lee did not want to go, but he could not disobey his father. His father's voice got weak. There was blood all over his body.

"Go now," he said. "And always remember: *Ua kom muaj zog. Zoo siab. Hais tias kog yog Hmoob.* Be strong. Be proud. You are Hmong." Then he died.

Lee made a bamboo raft. Then he hid in the jungle until nightfall. Finally he pushed the raft into the river and started the float to the other side. The water was warm. There was no moonlight and he crossed the river safely. He hid in the darkness until morning. Then he found a Thai farmer and asked for help.

"My name is LLLLLee," he said. To his horror, his tongue wouldn't work right. He tried it again. "My name is LLLLee."

He knew it was because of the soldiers and what they had done to his family. When he closed his eyes, he saw his dead mother. He remembered how she cared for him, how she loved him. And now she was gone.

"My nnnnname is LLLLLee," he said again.

Then he heard his father's last words again. He saw him bleeding to death in the grass and Lee's tongue wouldn't work right.

"PPPPPPlease help me," he told the Thai farmer. "My ffffffamily is all dddddead."

Part 2

Lee Vang found his clan in the refugee camp in Thailand. They took care of him. They comforted him when he thought about his dead family. He went to the camp school and learned English. Then he waited, like the others, to go to the United States.

But he still stammered and stuttered. Nothing would take it away and he was embarrassed to speak.

After a one-year wait in the refugee camp, Lee came to the United States. He started school and he was happy to be in America. Except for one thing: some of the kids in school laughed when he spoke.

The worst boy was William, a bully who rode the bus with Lee.

"Hey, LLLLLLLee!" William said every day. "LLLLLLLook, gggggggguys! It's LLLLLLLee, the cccccccchink!"

Lee hated this boy. William was big and had tough friends. He pushed everyone around. Each day he made Lee's life miserable. Lee wanted to join a gang, a Hmong gang. The first person he wanted to beat up was William. Lee wanted to teach him a lesson. He wanted to show William that he was tough, too; that he wasn't afraid.

VOCABULARY

embarrassed   ashamed
bully   a tough kid
chink   prejudiced name for Asians

Then something happened that changed all of that. Winter came. Slowly the roads filled with snow and ice. The bus driver had to be careful. One day the roads were very slippery and the kids were making lots of noise. William was the worst. He was out of his seat pushing another boy around. The driver turned around and told them to be quiet. The bus went off the road and turned over on its side. The driver hit his head and cried out in pain. The kids screamed and fell on top of one another.

Lee thought quickly, like he did the night the soldiers came. He climbed on top of the seat and reached up toward the windows, but the windows were stuck. Lee and the others were trapped like animals. The kids kept screaming, certain they were going to die. But Lee wasn't afraid. He tried the window again. The window still wouldn't move. Then he took his book bag and broke the glass. He covered his hand with his shirt, carefully picked out the glass still in the window, and threw it outside the bus. He helped the injured driver through the opening. Then he pulled himself out.

"Quickly!" he said, speaking in English. "Take my hand!" One by one, he pulled children to safety. William wanted to be first.

"Take me, Lee!" he said, pushing the other children away. Lee kicked him back into the bus. Lee hated him. Maybe today William would die.

Then the bus started on fire. Cars stopped and people took the children who were safely out away from the bus. Finally only William was left.

"LLLLLLLee!" William begged, looking at the fire. "HHHHHHelp mmmmmme!"

Lee spit on him. "You *still* make fun of me? Then today you die."

"PPPPPlease," William said, "I cccccccan't help it. MMMMMy tongue dddddoesn't wwwwork rrrrrright."

Lee saw the terror in William's face. It was the terror of death. Lee had faced that terror once, on the Mekong River, and today he was no longer afraid of it.

"Quickly," he said to William, taking his arm and pulling him out of the burning bus. William couldn't speak because he was shaking so badly. Lee jumped from the bus to safety.

Part 3

One week later, the school principal gave Lee Vang an award. Newspaper people took his picture and the mayor shook his hand. They asked Lee to give a speech and he spoke with a strong voice. His tongue worked fine. He told them about the Hmong people and their struggle to get to the United States and everyone listened. He told them about walking through the jungle and crossing the Mekong River and watching his parents die and eating canned sardines in the refugee camp, and now he was here in the United States and he was going to make it here. Everyone in school respected the Hmong students now. Then he remembered his father's words and he turned to his Hmong friends and said:

"*Peb tau los deb lawm hov ntau.* We have come a long way. *Ntawm no tsis yog peb lub tsev.* This is not our home. *Tab si peb yuav tsum ua kom nws yog peb lub tsev.* But we must make it our home. *Qhov ua rau kog nyuaj siab, nco ntsoor ib yam:* In your struggle remember one thing: *Ua kom muaj zog. Zoo siab. Hais tias koj yog Hmoob.* Be strong. Be proud. You are Hmong."

Responding to Reading

Sharing Ideas

1. Courage can be expressed inwardly (inside ourselves), or outwardly (among other people). Talk about the different people in these stories. How do they express courage? What is courage? What is the word for "courage" in your language?

2. Discuss personality traits courageous people have in common.

3. Share a story of courage from your own life with your class.

4. Find information on the Chernobyl disaster. Try looking in the library for newspaper or magazine articles. Why do you think the government kept this event a secret?

5. Discuss: Should the United States government give the Black Hills back to the Lakota people? Research and discuss laws that could preserve or restore Native American lands and rights.

6. Look for books, pictures, or articles that have stereotypical views of Native Americans. What is wrong with these English phrases: "Indian giver" and "Sit like an Indian"?

7. Watch the movie, *The Killing Fields*. Talk about your reactions.

Writing About Courage

1. Write about a time when you were afraid. What happened? Who was there? Where were you?

2. Write about a story of courage in your life or in the life of someone you know.

3. Write a letter of hope and encouragement to Vika Ivchenko.

4. Native American people were forced to leave their homes and live on reservations. Often they could only take what they could carry on their back. Pretend that you have just learned that you have to leave your home. You have to leave in two days. Make a list of the things you would take. Remember, you can only take things you can carry.

5. Summarize the history of the Hmong people. Where are they from? What are they like? What is their language like? If possible, interview a Hmong person in your school.

6. In the story "The Video Arcade," Sok and his friends play games. Make a list of the popular games and sports in your culture. Think of board games, card games, professional sports, types of gambling, and games you played as a child. Explain each game to the class. How does each game reflect your culture? (For example, Monopoly, in the United States.)

More Reading

The Little Weaver of Thai-Yen Village, Khanh Tuyet Tran. Children's Book Press, 1987.

Black Elk, a Man with a Vision, Carol Greene. Children's Press, 1990.

Fighters, Refugees, Immigrants: A Story of the Hmong, Mace Goldfarb. Carolrhoda Press, 1982.

A Migrant Family, Larry Dane Brimmer. Lerner Publications, 1992.

Going Home, Nicholasa Mohr. Dial Books, 1986.

Dark Sky, Dark Land, David Moore. Tessera Publishing, 1989.

Number the Stars, Lois Lowry. Houghton Mifflin Company, 1989.

Journey to Jo'burg, Beverly Naidoo. J.B. Lippincott, 1985.

The Land I Lost, Adventures of a Boy in Vietnam, Huynh Quang Nhuong. Harper and Row, 1982.

Becoming Americans: Asian Sojourners, Immigrants, Refugees, Tricia Knoll. Coast to Coast Books, 1982.

Hill of Fire, Thomas Lewis. Harper and Row, 1971.

Tales of Prejudice

You may write me down in history
With your bitter, twisted lies.
You may trod me in the very dirt
But still, like dust, I'll rise.

> *Maya Angelou*
> *African American writer*

The Dust of Life

The girl in this story is an Amerasian child. Her father is an American soldier. Her mother is a Vietnamese woman. She wants to find her father, but first she must overcome prejudice.

Part 1

"*Bui doi!*" the other children said. "*Bui doi!*"

Little Thuy cried. She didn't know why the other children hated her.

"Grandma," she said one night, "what does *bui doi* mean? Why do the other kids call me that?"

"There was a war," her grandmother said. "American soldiers were here. Many children were born. They had American fathers and Vietnamese mothers. Many times there was no marriage. The children are half American and half Vietnamese. People here call these children *bui doi*. It means 'the dust of life.'"

"Were my father and mother married?"

"Yes," the grandmother said, but she didn't know.

"Your mother was killed by soldiers. She was a teacher. Your father is in the United States. His name is James. That is all I know."

That night Thuy cried herself to sleep.

"Father," she said, "I only want to know you. I only want to hear the sound of your voice. I won't eat much. I won't be a bother. I'll cook for you. I'll clean for you. I only want to love you."

One day a Vietnamese man came to the house. He wanted to see Thuy. He said he was a relative of Thuy. Thuy's grandmother had never seen him before. All of Thuy's relatives were dead.

VOCABULARY

hate   strong dislike
dust   powdered dirt
bother   a nuisance
no fool   not stupid
fake   false; not real
tien   Vietnamese money

"I want to take her to the United States," the man said, "I can help her find her father."

The grandmother was no fool. She read the newspapers. The United States was letting Amerasian children come to America. The whole family of an Amerasian child could come to the United States also. Now everyone in Vietnam wanted an Amerasian child. The child was the ticket to America.

The grandmother thought to herself. I am old now. What will Thuy do when I die? Who will care for her? Will she live on the street like the other Amerasian children? Maybe she should go to the United States with this man. Maybe she could find her father.

"Do you have a wife?" the grandmother asked the man.

"Yes," he said.

"Do you have children?"

"Three," he said.

"Show me something that says you are Thuy's relative."

He handed her a paper. The paper said he was Thuy's uncle. She knew it was fake. Anyone with money could get such a paper.

"Ten thousand tien," the grandmother said.

"What!" the man screamed.

"Ten thousand!" the grandmother said again. "You heard me! Otherwise get out of my house."

The man spit on the ground and left.

Two days later, however, he returned.

"Here," he said, handing the grandmother the money. "We leave in two weeks."

"Will you find her father?" the grandmother said.

"I promise," the man said.

The next day the grandmother made a new dress for Thuy. She sewed the money into the dress.

"Thuy," she said, "this dress is for you. Touch here. There's money hidden here. Don't tell anyone. In two weeks you're going to the United States. Your father is waiting for you. He loves you and wants to see you. I am old. There is nothing for you here. You must go."

That night Thuy cried lonely tears. How could she leave her grandmother? Her grandmother was old. She wanted to care for her. But she had to go. She couldn't disobey her grandmother. But maybe now she would know her father.

"Father," she said again, as she fell asleep, "I only want to know you. I only want to hear the sound of your voice. I won't eat much. I won't be a bother. I'll cook for you. I'll clean for you. I only want to love you."

Part 2

Two weeks later, Thuy left Vietnam. The airplane frightened her. Her new family would not talk to her. They made her sit by herself. When they landed in America, they let her get off the plane first. They smiled at her now. They stroked her hair lovingly.

"This is Thuy," her uncle told the immigration person. "She is Amerasian, see?" He showed them her papers. "We are her family."

Thuy was frightened of San Francisco. She had never seen any place like it before.

"We will only stay here a few days," her uncle said.

Two days later he took Thuy to a bus station.

"Here is your ticket," he said. "When the bus stops, wait for us there, and we will join you."

Her uncle left. The bus drove away. Thuy was alone. No one spoke her language on the bus. She didn't know where she was going. She thought of her father and she cried softly to herself.

"Father," she said, "I only want to know you. I only want to hear the sound of your voice. I won't eat much. I won't be a bother. I'll cook for you. I'll clean for you. I only want to love you."

Finally, the bus stopped.

"LAST STOP!" the bus driver said. "EVERYONE OFF!"

Thuy did not understand. But she left when the others did. Alone, in a strange town, she sat on a bench and cried.

A police officer came up to her. She was extremely frightened. The police she knew beat people. They robbed people. They were like soldiers.

"Why are you crying?" the police officer asked. His voice was kind. Thuy looked down. She didn't dare look him in the eye.

"Do you need help?" the police officer asked. "Are you all right?"

Thuy could not understand anything.

"Please come with me," the police officer said.

Thuy cried harder now. She was alone in the car with the police officer. They drove to the government center. A kind woman talked to Thuy. She said she was a social worker, but Thuy did not understand her words. The social worker gave her food and a warm place to sleep that night.

Part 3

The next morning the social worker came to see Thuy again. But this time there was a Vietnamese woman with her. Thuy was overwhelmed with joy.

"*Ten em la gi?* What is your name?" the woman asked.

"Thuy Nguyen."

"*Em den my khi nao?* When did you come to the United States?"

"*Mai may ngay truoc.* Only a few days ago."

"*Em den vai ai?* Who did you come with?"

"*Vai ngaai dan ong ma ong noi rang ong la chu cua em.* A man who said he was my uncle. He said he would find my father."

"*Ong ay dau roi?* Where is this man now?"

"San Francisco."

"*Lam sao em tai duoc cai tinh nho nay?* How did you get to this small town?"

"*Ong any cho em di xe do va bao em dai o day.* He put me on a bus and told me to wait here."

The Vietnamese woman's face saddened. She knew the man had used Thuy to get to the United States. Now he had abandoned her.

"*Anh co biet gi ve gia dinh cua anh o Vietnam khong?* Do you know anything about your family in Vietnam?" the woman asked. "*Chung toi co the tim bo anh.* Maybe we can find your father."

Thuy took the money out of her dress. Inside the money was a piece of paper. It had her father's name on it. It had her mother's name and the date of Thuy's birth. It had everything her grand-

VOCABULARY

overwhelmed with joy very happy

abandon to leave alone

mother knew about Thuy's father. The woman took the paper and translated it for the social worker. The social worker wrote everything down.

"*Lam on a lai voi gia dinh chung toi.* Please stay with my family," the Vietnamese woman said kindly. "*Nguoi dan ba nay se co gang tim bo anh.* This woman will try to find your father."

Days went by. Weeks went by. Thuy started school. She learned English. She waited and waited, but her father never came. The rain on the window was like the tears in her heart. The wind in the trees blew dry and empty. The beautiful flowers had no fragrance. Always she whispered the same thing at night as she fell asleep:

"Father, I only want to know you. I only want to hear the sound of your voice. I won't eat much. I won't be a bother. I'll cook for you. I'll clean for you. I only want to love you."

Then one day, when Thuy had lost hope, there was a knock on the door. It was the social worker. A man was with her.

"Thuy?" the man said softly. "Are you Thuy?"

"Yes."

"I am your father. Here is a picture of your mother. For years, I have whispered in my sleep: 'Daughter, I only want to know you. I only want to love you and care for you. Please come home.'"

The Poor Woman's Gift

Anandi Gopal had no more rice. Now her family had nothing to eat. Where was Swami Chandra when she needed him? For years she had filled his begging bowl with rice. Now, just when she needed him, his gate was locked. Where was he?

Part 1

Once there was a poor woman in India named Anandi Gopal. She lived in Bombay. Her husband was sick with malaria and unable to work, so she sold paper flowers on the street.

For five days Anandi had not sold a flower. Her family was hungry. Tomorrow the last of their rice would be gone. When darkness came to Bombay she walked home slowly. She didn't have one rupee in her sari. Then she remembered Swami Chandra, a kind swami who lived nearby, and she decided to ask him for help.

Anandi knocked on his gate, but the gate was locked. She thought of her hungry family and became angry.

"Where is Swami Chandra?" she hollered, "And why is his gate locked? My family is hungry and he's supposed to take care of us."

"Maybe he isn't in today," another woman said.

"Isn't in?" Anandi replied, banging loudly on the gate, "Is that what you think? Can't you read? The sign says he's supposed to receive visitors now."

The woman hurried away.

"A kind swami?" Anandi hollered, calling to the woman. "Is that what you think? Well, I don't think he's so kind. How many years have we given *him* food when *he* was hungry? Now *my* family is hungry. Where is he?"

VOCABULARY

Bombay   a large city in India
malaria   a disease caused by a mosquito
rupee   Indian money
sari   the dress of an Indian woman
swami   a Hindu priest
begging bowl   the bowl Hindu priests use to beg for food

Part 2

Anandi went home. That evening she cooked the last rice and gave it to her family. Her children cried for more food and she thought of Swami Chandra again.

"Why do people give him food?" she said bitterly. "He sits around all day doing nothing. Then he begs for food from people too poor to feed their own families. Tomorrow I'm going to visit him again. This time I'm going to bring *my* begging bowl to *him*."

The next morning came. Anandi didn't sell one flower all day.

Now there was nothing left to feed her family, not even a few grains of rice.

"SWAMI!" she hollered, banging on Swami Chandra's gate again. "I'M BACK WITH MY BEGGING BOWL. COME OUT. TONIGHT MY CHILDREN WILL SLEEP WITH NOTHING IN THEIR STOMACHS. OPEN THE GATE OR I'LL BREAK IT DOWN!"

Inside there was only silence. Anandi kicked the gate. She beat it with her fists and threw stones at it. But still there was only silence. Finally she left.

That evening her children cried with hunger. She had nothing to give them, not even one grain of rice. She listened to their cries and then left the house. Outside on a dark Bombay street, skinny dogs poked through the garbage looking for food.

"I will become like a dog," she said, "and look through the garbage for food." She walked through the garbage on the street and picked up tiny bits of food and put them in her sari. She didn't dare raise her head, so great was her shame. Then she started home.

Part 3

After walking a short distance, Anandi stopped. Somewhere children were crying. Were they her children? No. The cries came from someplace else. They were pitiful cries, too. They came from a poor shack in an alley. The tiny shack was made of cardboard and had a tin roof. No one ever visited the family because they were Muslim.

VOCABULARY

shack   very shabby house
burlap   cloth
stooped   bend over
huddled   sit closely
Allah   Muslim word for "God"

Anandi walked down the dark alley to the tiny shack. There was no door, only a burlap rag to keep the dogs away at night.

"Hello," Anandi called. She waited for an answer.

Finally someone said in a weak voice, "Enter."

Anandi parted the burlap and stooped through the opening. Three children without clothes huddled around a woman in rags. They were all crowded around a tiny candle, their only source of heat and light. On the dirt floor, their grandmother lay dying. She was lying on cold burlap and her body was a skeleton. There were open sores on her side.

"Woman," Anandi whispered, barely able to speak, "when was the last time your family ate?"

"I can't remember," the woman said.

"Where is your husband?"

"He is dead."

"Do you have any relatives?"

"None. Each day I pray to Allah that we may die."

Anandi looked at the shivering children. Their hair was dirty and matted. Their stomachs were swollen and they were dying of hunger.

Part 4

Anandi left the shack and walked home. Her tiny house looked large and warm now. Her husband looked healthy. Her children had plump cheeks and smooth skin.

Her husband handed her a package. "Here," he said.

"Where did you get this rice?" Anandi asked.

"Does it matter?" her husband answered.

"You stole it, didn't you? What if the police come?"

"They can take it from our bellies." Her husband laughed.

VOCABULARY

plump   fat
nourishing food   healthy food

Anandi opened the bag of rice and heated the fire. Then she cooked the rice and fed her family. But when she saw the nourishing food she thought about the poor Muslim family living in the dark alley.

Does it matter if a child is Muslim or Hindu? she thought. No, the cry of hunger is the same. She took a large spoon and put half the rice into another bowl. Then she left.

When she returned, her husband asked, "Where did you go?"

"To visit a family poorer than us."

"Which family?"

"The one in the alley. They have only a burlap rag to keep the dogs out at night."

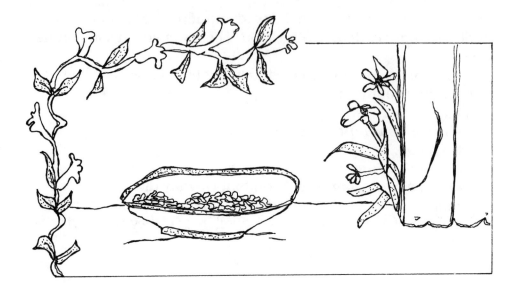

"But they are Muslim," her husband said. "I didn't steal to feed Muslims."

"Hush," Anandi said. "The cry of hunger is the same."

Part 5

The next day a busload of tourists came to the Banyon Hotel, a five-star hotel in Bombay. Anandi made 30 rupees selling flowers, enough money to feed her family for a week. On her way home, she was so happy she decided to visit Swami Chandra. She wanted to tell him that her family was all right now. She was so happy that her bare feet danced on the Bombay street. Even the monsoon rain felt warm now. To her great joy, Swami Chandra's gate was open.

VOCABULARY

five-star the most expensive
monsoon heavy seasonal rain in India
japa a Hindu form of prayer

"Gardener," she said, "may I please see Swami today?"

"I'm sorry," the gardener said, "Swami is sleeping. He's been saying japa for three days and hasn't slept or eaten. A poor Muslim family is dying nearby. They haven't eaten for weeks. They have only a burlap rag to keep the dogs away at night."

Now Anandi knew why Swami Chandra's gate had been locked.

"This morning the grandmother died," the gardener said. "Her poor body was full of sores. But the mother and children will live. Last night a kind neighbor brought them food."

Anandi walked home. There was money in her sari for rice. There were fresh flowers in her hand from Swami Chandra's garden. They would bring a good price tomorrow at the Banyon Hotel. Half the money would go to the Muslim family until they were well.

The Slave Poet

The Story of Phillis Wheatley

What would you do if you were taken from your parents as a small child and sold into slavery? What would you do if you were brought to another country, did not know the language, and were forbidden to go to school? In this true story of prejudice, a small black girl overcomes loss of family, loss of homeland, slavery, illness, and illiteracy and becomes a famous poet.

Phillis Wheatley was born in 1753 in Senegal, West Africa. When she was eight she was kidnapped and sold into slavery. She was put on a slave ship, without her parents, and taken to the United States.

John Wheatley, a Northern white business man, bought her at a slave auction. She became a servant of the Wheatley family. Fortunately, the family treated her kindly. Phillis loved poetry and when the Wheatleys

VOCABULARY

kidnapped stolen
slave auction slave sale
stunned very surprised
boarding house hotel

realized that she was gifted, they taught her to read and write.

Phillis started writing poetry when she was 14. Many people read her poems and were stunned that a black slave girl who had just learned to read and write had such talent.

When Phillis was 20 she became sick. The Wheatleys freed her from slavery and sent her to England to get well. A publishing company in London saw her poems and published them in a book called *Poems on Various Subjects, Religious and Moral.*

Phillis Wheatley got better and returned to the United States. The entire Wheatley family was sick now and she took care of them. Within a few years, the Wheatley family died.

Phillis married John Peters, a freed slave. He stole her second book before it could be printed and used it to pay his debts. He ended up in a debtor's prison and Phillis's second book was never published.

Phillis went to work in a boarding house. It was exhausting work and she died at age 31. She is remembered as one of the first African American poets in the United States.

Ryan's Story

AIDS is a terrifying disease which destroys the immune system. In this true story a small boy gets AIDS from infected blood. When he returns to school, he experiences cruel prejudice. Before he dies, however, he touches the hearts of people in the United States and inspires thousands of people to overcome their fear of AIDS.

Part 1

Once there was a boy named Ryan White. He was born in 1971 in Kokomo, Indiana. Three days after his birth, doctors discovered that he had hemophilia, a disease which prevents the blood from clotting. To save his life they gave Ryan injections of Factor VII.

Ryan had a normal childhood until he was 12. Then he started to get sick. Off and on he had diarrhea, stomach cramps, night sweats, exhaustion, fever, coughing, and finally severe pneumonia which almost took his life.

Doctors took a blood test and found that Ryan had AIDS. He had gotten AIDS from infected Factor VII which he took for hemophilia. For months Ryan was too weak to go to school. Doctors did not think he would live more than six months.

However, Ryan got better. He wanted to go back to school and be with his friends and live a normal life. But the school would not let him return. The parents, teachers, and other children were afraid that Ryan would give them AIDS.

AIDS was a new disease then, and everyone feared it. There was much false information about AIDS. People thought AIDS could be spread by casual contact like touches, sneezes, kisses, sweat, or tears. Doctors told the people of Kokomo that AIDS could not be spread this way, but they still would not let Ryan come back to school.

Ryan and his mother sued the school. For nine months there was a legal fight. During this time Ryan had to stay home. Finally, a judge said Ryan could return to school.

When he returned to school, however, he experienced cruel prejudice. All of his friends left him. Kids called him a "fag." They told cruel jokes to his face and laughed at him. Nobody would touch him. They broke into his school locker and took his things. They said he spit on vegetables to give people AIDS. They said he bit people to give them AIDS. He had to use a separate drinking fountain and a separate bathroom. He could not go to gym class.

VOCABULARY

hemophilia a disease in which bleeding does not stop

injections shots of medicine given with a needle

Factor VII a liquid made from human blood which helps the blood to clot

clot stop bleeding

infected diseased

fag slang word for "homo-sexual"

disposable plates plates made to be thrown away

Nobody would be his lab partner in science class. He had to use disposable plates when he ate in the cafeteria. People wrote cruel articles in the newspaper. They threw garbage on his lawn. They tried to have Ryan taken away from his mother by the court. Some parents removed their children and started their own private school.

Ryan would not quit school, however. Each day he went to school. He said he did not want to sit home and die of AIDS. He wanted to go to school and live a normal life. At times he was very sick and his mother thought he was dying. But each time he got better. Ryan said, "If you think about dying, it only makes it worse. If you think about living, you will get better."

Ryan kept thinking positive thoughts. He said, "If I can live long enough, maybe they will find a cure for AIDS." He said, "I'm going to beat this disease or I'm going to die trying." He was not bitter at his friends and the people of Kokomo. He said, "They are just ignorant about AIDS and how it is spread. They are doing these cruel things because they are afraid."

Part 2

Ryan's private life was gone now. He was famous as "the boy with AIDS who could not return to school" and reporters from all over the country called and bothered his family. Some stayed for days trying to get their story. Over 50 "faith healers" said they could heal him. Dozens of boxes came in the mail with "secret potions" from people he didn't know. This was exhausting for Ryan and his mother.

Ryan became a national symbol of the prejudice surrounding AIDS. Many stars like Elton John and Michael Jackson became his friends and helped him. Ryan gave speeches about AIDS when he was strong enough to talk. Sometimes the speeches were to small groups of students. Sometimes they were to large groups. One speech was to 10,000 teachers in the Superdome in New Orleans. He spoke to Congress in Washington, D. C. about AIDS. He became a poster boy for AIDS education in the United States. A movie, called *The Ryan White Story,* was made about his life. He had a part in the movie and worked on the set every day, even though he was very sick at times.

His doctor said, "Ryan White should have died years ago. But Ryan is special. He wants to live. He wants to go to school and have a normal life. He wants to help people understand this terrible disease. He wants people to know that anybody can get AIDS, not just drug users and homosexuals."

Ryan said, "Some people still think AIDS is spread through the air, so they don't want to be in the same room with me, and it hurts. But I'm going to try to change their minds. They ask the same questions over and over and I try to be patient. But ignorance dies hard. This is going to take a lot longer than I ever dreamed."

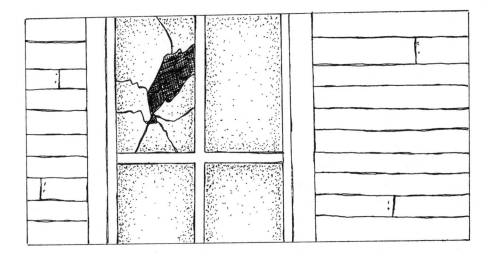

Then one day a terrible thing happened in Kokomo. Someone shot a bullet into Ryan's house. His family got so terrified they moved away.

Part 3

Ryan moved to the small town of Cicero, Indiana. One day there was a knock on the door.

"Hi," someone said. "My name is Jill Stewart. I'm your neighbor." Ryan couldn't believe it. A neighbor, and someone his own age, had actually come to see him? Nobody ever came to see him. He had no friends. Yes, famous people were his friends, but everyone his own age in school had left him.

"I'm also the president of the student body at Hamilton Heights High School," the girl said. "I want to welcome you to our school and tell you nobody will treat you badly. We want everything to be normal."

Ryan couldn't believe it. The kids wanted him in school? His neighbors wanted him? A pretty girl his own age, and the president of the student body, wanted to be his friend? He didn't know what to say. It had been so long since anyone had treated him normally.

"I'll second that," Ryan finally said.

Ryan's life in Cicero was happy. His new school started an AIDS education program. The school answered all the questions that students had about AIDS. If someone was still frightened, they could visit a counselor in school. If someone was afraid to ask a question, there was a box to put your question in without your name.

Then the students wrote letters in the newspaper and spoke at churches in the town. They discovered that AIDS education is most effective when it begins with the students and not the parents. When the parents of one student wanted to remove their child from the school, the student said "No."

The students and parents knew that AIDS could not be spread through the air. They were not afraid of Ryan and they wanted to be his friend. His new friends rode to school with him in the morning. They wanted to sit with him in the lunchroom at school. They did things together in the evening, like normal teenagers. Everyone wanted to talk to him and hear stories about Elton John and Michael Jackson and the famous people that Ryan knew. But they also wanted to be friends with Ryan, just because he was Ryan White, a nice person. Even the school janitor liked Ryan. One day the janitor handed Ryan this poem that he had written for Ryan:

Ryan's Poem

We are sorry for your fight
But for every day that you are here
We can see a little light.

Ryan was 16 now. He was only five feet tall and weighed 90 pounds. AIDS was destroying his body. But Ryan White, the person inside his tiny body, still wanted to live. He got a job in a store that sold skateboards. "My first job!" he said. "My first paycheck!" He bought clothes.

But he was very sick. He needed a hair dryer to keep his hands and feet warm. He threw up. He rattled when he breathed. He ran out of breath when he spoke. He was weak and exhausted. His stomach swelled. He was put in the hospital again. On the way, he passed the Cicero cemetery.

"Not yet!" he laughed, "Not yet! I'll get better!"

In the hospital he thought about the party at Disneyland that Elton John had given him and he got better. Elton had hugged him and shared food with him to show people not to be afraid of Ryan.

For the next two years Ryan became sicker and weaker. Thousands of people wrote him letters of love and support. Dozens of famous people talked to him and encouraged him. Michael Jackson gave him a car. Elton John invited him to his concerts and sang to him on stage.

Everyone wanted Ryan White to overcome AIDS. But in April, 1990, Ryan became very sick again. He was in Los Angeles for a television show. He barely made it through the show. He had long coughing spells. He had a hernia and could hardly speak. He had a fever. His throat was raw and sore.

He told his mother he wanted to go home. Jeanie White was afraid Ryan was dying this time. They returned to his doctor in Indiana. Ryan was put in the hospital again. Everything inside him seemed to be breaking down.

His last phone call was to his grandmother in Florida.

"Grandma," he said, "remember when we were small and we used to write our ABCs in the sand, and the waves would come and wash it away?"

"Yes," his grandmother said. "They were beautiful ABCs, too."

Ryan became too weak to speak so he wrote notes. The doctor wanted to put tubes down his throat and put him in an oxygen tent. Ryan wrote, "Go for it," on a piece of paper.

"Everything is going to be all right, honey," his mother whispered.

Ryan wrote one more note. "Mom?" he wrote. He was barely able to move his fingers. Then he went unconscious.

For one week Ryan was unconscious. Hundreds of people from around the country called the hospital. Hundreds of people sent cards and gifts. His friends from Hamilton Heights High School came to visit. Elton John stayed at the hospital with Ryan's mother.

Finally, Ryan's blood pressure dropped. Ryan White was dying. Jeanie White looked at her son's tiny body inside the oxygen tent. Then she looked at Ryan's face and she knew that his long struggle was finally over.

"Just let go, Ryan," she whispered. "It's all right, sweetheart."

Part 4

Ryan White died on April 8, 1990. It was Palm Sunday morning. His funeral was the largest Indiana had ever seen. Fifteen hundred people crowded into the church and long lines of people waited outside to walk by his casket. Ryan was dressed like the normal schoolboy he wanted to be. He was wearing his jeans, his jean jacket, a surf shirt, sneakers, his sunglasses, and the watch Michael Jackson had given him. Two hundred and fifty cars followed the hearse to the cemetery in Cicero, Indiana.

At the funeral the choir from Hamilton Heights High School stood around his casket and sang "That's What Friends Are For," a song written to raise money for AIDS research.

Elton John sang "Skyline Pigeon," a song about a bird flying toward freedom. Elton had a heart made of 250 red roses placed around Ryan's casket. The ribbon on the heart said, "Dear Ryan,

VOCABULARY

Palm Sunday a Christian religious day

casket a body is placed in a casket for burial

hearse the car that carries the casket to the cemetery

you will always be with me. You have touched many people. Thank you. I love you. Elton."

Ryan White died with no bitterness toward those who feared his disease. He overcame prejudice. Many people visit his grave in Cicero, Indiana. They leave flowers, poems, toys, and friendship bracelets. His minister said, "Ryan White helped to make AIDS a disease and not a dirty word."

Scratch the Wind

Child abuse? How could anyone suspect her loving parents of child abuse? But that's what happened to Souphaphone Keohanam, the new girl from Laos. It was all part of her first confusing week of school in the United States.

Part 1

Miss Jackson was a new teacher at Washington School. Her students liked her. She was warm and friendly. She let the students read interesting books and write in diaries and take trips and go outside on warm days. Some days she read funny stories to them and they all laughed.

One day a new girl came to class.

"This is Souphaphone Keohanam," Miss Jackson said. "She's from Laos." Miss Jackson pulled down the map of the world and touched Laos with a wooden pointer. "She speaks and writes the Laotian language. This is how you write 'hello' in her language." Miss Jackson wrote funny lines on the blackboard.

ສະບາຍດີ

The students looked at Souphaphone. She was quiet. She had black hair and a round face. Her shoes were new and didn't have a spot of dirt on them.

"Yuk!" one boy said, laughing. "She's funny looking!"

VOCABULARY

the office   where the principal works
welfare   money from the government
Asian flu   a disease
AIDS   a disease with no cure
make a fuss over   pay a lot of attention to someone

"Peter!" Miss Jackson said sharply. She was very angry. The students had never seen Miss Jackson this angry. "Go to the office!"

"My dad says they're taking our jobs," a girl said.

"Susan!" Miss Jackson said. "Go to the office!"

"My dad says they're all on welfare," another girl said.

"Andrea!" Miss Jackson said. "Go to the office!"

"My mom says they have big families so they can receive more welfare," a girl said.

"Amy!" Miss Jackson said. "Go to the office!"

"My brother says they eat their own pets," a boy said.

"Andrew!" Miss Jackson said. "Go to the office!"

"My brother says they brought Asian flu and AIDS to the United States," a boy said.

"James!" Miss Jackson said. "Go to the office!"

"My brother says they drive new cars and have fancy stereos, but they don't have any furniture," a girl said.

"Mary!" Miss Jackson said. "Go to the office!"

Finally, there were only two people left in the room, Miss Jackson and Souphaphone.

"What are those marks on your arm?" Miss Jackson said. Souphaphone had bruises on her arm. "Oh, my goodness!" Miss Jackson said. "Child abuse! We both have to go to the office!"

They walked down the hallway together and Miss Jackson wondered about Asian people. Somebody said they hit their children in the old country. That's why their children were so quiet and so well behaved and why they never talked back to their parents or to their teachers. Miss Jackson didn't believe it at first, but now she wondered.

Souphaphone followed quietly by Miss Jackson's side. The whole week had been confusing to her. Who were these strange people who all looked alike? Why were they making such a fuss over her? Where was the bathroom? Why did the kids laugh at her? Why was the teacher angry? Why did everyone talk so loud? Why did everyone look her in the eye? Why did people touch her on the top of the head? How would she ever get used to the food in the lunchroom? She heard there was another Asian girl somewhere in one of the other classes. If only she could find her, then everything would be all right.

Part 2

Two days later, Miss Jackson was talking to her class.

"Peter," she said sternly, "do you have your assignment done?"

"Yes, Miss Jackson," Peter said.

"Very well. Read it to us, then."

"We are just as funny-looking to Asian people as they are to us," Peter read. "We all look alike to them."

"Susan," Miss Jackson said, "your turn."

"In most cases, Asian immigrants begin with jobs that no one else wants. Often they are discriminated against. They receive low pay and suffer from poor working conditions."

"Andrea," Miss Jackson said.

"Many Asians do begin with assistance, but statistics show they soon become self-supporting."

"Amy," Miss Jackson said.

"Large families are part of Asian people's history and culture."

"Andrew," Miss Jackson said.

"Most Southeast Asians do not have pets in their homes and they do not eat their pets."

"James," Miss Jackson said.

"According to the State Health Department, neither Asian flu nor AIDS is caused by Southeast Asians."

"Mary," Miss Jackson said.

VOCABULARY

sternly very seriously
assignment homework
immigrants people from other countries
discriminated against treated badly
assistance financial help
pool their money save together

"Southeast Asian families often pool their money to buy things and then they share them. They usually pay in cash and do not like credit card debt."

"Very good, class," Miss Jackson said. "And now it's my turn, because I learned something, too. Two days ago I brought Souphaphone to the office. There were bruises on her arm. I thought someone had hurt her. But I learned something. Do you see this bottle? It's full of oil. Asian people call it 'Tiger Balm oil.' I'm going to pass it around and I want everyone to put some of it on their arm. Now take one of these spoons. Turn your spoon upside down and scratch yourself with it. Harder. Rub the spoon on the oil. Do you see the red mark on your skin? Now feel the mark. Is it hot? Asian people sometimes scratch themselves with a spoon when they are sick. This lets heat out of the body and makes them feel better. The marks on Souphaphone's arm were caused by a spoon. Her parents were trying to care for her in their own way. Lao people call it 'scratch the wind.'"

Responding to Reading

Sharing Ideas

1. "Prejudice" means "to prejudge." It means to form an opinion of someone before you meet them, usually a negative opinion. Discuss examples of prejudice in these stories.

2. Discuss the different forms of prejudice. How is prejudice passed from parents to children?

3. How does television contribute to prejudice? What television shows or commercials have you seen that suggest prejudicial attitudes? For example, "Thin is beautiful," or "Youth is beautiful."

4. Think of words that are racist: "chink," "nigger," "wop," "redskins," "gook." What other words can you think of? What do they mean? Who started them? Why?

5. Think of ideas that are prejudiced. ("Men don't know how to care for small children." "Mexican people in the United States are all illegal aliens." "All Asians are smart in math.") What other prejudice ideas can you think of? How did they start? Who do they hurt?

6. Perform a small play about prejudice. Select writers, a director, actresses and actors, stage hands. What is your message?

7. In the story "The Poor Woman's Gift," what was her gift? Why was the gate open at the end of the story, but closed at the beginning? Discuss three things you know about India after reading this story.

8. Imagine that you are Thuy. You find your father. What will you say to him?

9. In the story "Scratch the Wind," Souphaphone is confused by the way people act. She wonders why they look her in the eye and touch her on the head. Have you ever felt this way? Discuss other people's actions that seem unusual to you. What do you think these actions mean?

Writing About Prejudice

1. Have you ever experienced prejudice? Write about it. What happened? How did it feel? What was your emotional reaction? What is the answer to prejudice?

2. Think of strong ideas in your culture (ideas about men, women, power, family, children, divorce, sex, illness, religion, death). Are any of these ideas prejudicial? Before we can accept another culture, what ideas do we have to give up?

3. In the story "Scratch The Wind," the girl is new in school. Write about your first day or week of school in the United States. What do you remember? What was confusing to you? Who helped you? What would you do to make it easier for others?

4. Keep a journal for one week. List any forms of prejudice you see. Consider television, radio, friends, school, and newspaper stories. List prejudicial language, clothes, male/female roles, and professions.

5. Imagine you are the main character in any of these stories. Try to rewrite the story as that person.

6. Write a letter to Ryan White. If you visited his grave, would you leave anything?

7. Imagine you just received the news that you are HIV positive. Write a letter to the person you love the most telling them the news. How would you plan your life out?

8. You are the Surgeon General of the United States. You are responsible for the health of the citizens of the United States. Write a letter to the people of the United States. What will you tell them about AIDS?

More Reading

Great Women in the Struggle: A Book of Black Heroes, Toyomi Ignus. Just Us Books, 1991.

Nettie's Trip South, Ann Turner. Macmillan, 1987.

The Magic Paper, Tana Reiff. Fearon/Janus/Quercus, 1989.

Nobody Knows, Tana Reiff. Fearon/Janus/Quercus, 1989.

Journey to Jo'burg, Beverly Naidoo. J.P. Lippincott, 1985.

The Island on Bird Street, Uri Orlev. Houghton Mifflin, 1984.

Happily May I Walk: American Indians and Alaska Natives Today, Arlene Hirschfelder. Charles Scribner's Sons, 1986.

Phillis Wheatley and Her Writings, William Robinson. Garland, 1984.

Ryan White, My Own Story, Ryan White and Ann Marie Cunningham. Dial Books, 1991.

Imagining America: Paul Thai's Journey from the Killing Fields of Cambodia to Freedom in the U.S.A., Sharon Sloan Fiffer. Paragon House, 1991.

Hearts of Sorrow, Vietnamese American Lives, James Freeman. Stanford University Press, 1991.

We Remember the Holocaust, David Adler. Henry Holt, 1989.

Tales of Long Ago

Tell me the tales that to me were so dear,
Long, long ago, long, long ago.

Thomas Haynes Bayly

The Clever Judge

A Russian folktale

In this folktale a man commits a crime. The judge tricks the criminal. It is a "trickery" folktale.

Once there was a wise man. He was famous for justice and wisdom. People came from all over to have him settle their disputes.

One day two villagers came. The wise man said, "What do you want to tell me?"

"Well," the first man said, "Last week I left our village on business. I had one hundred gold coins in my house. I had worked hard for them. I did not want to carry the coins with me, nor did I want them stolen while I was gone. So I asked this man to watch the coins for me. When I returned, the coins were gone and he said I never gave them to him."

"Who saw you give him the money?" the wise judge asked.

"No one saw it. We went into the forest and there I handed him the coins."

The judge looked at the other man. "What do you have to say about this?"

"I don't know what he's talking about," the other man said. "I never went into the forest with him and I never saw any gold coins."

The judge looked back at the first man.

"Do you remember the place where you handed him the coins?"

"Yes. It was under a tall oak tree. I remember the tree very well. I can find it with no trouble at all."

"Then there was a witness," the judge said. "Go to the oak tree and ask the tree to come here and verify your story."

The man left quickly for the forest.

The judge waited and waited. Finally he lost patience. He turned to the other man and said with anger, "Where do you think he is? Hasn't he reached the oak tree by now?"

"No, not yet," the man said.

They waited longer. The judge was furious. "Now do you think he's reached the oak tree?"

"Yes," the man said, "By now he must have reached it."

Finally, the first man returned from the forest. He was tired and out of breath.

"Well?" the judge asked.

"The tree won't come to see you," the man said.

"Never mind," the judge said. "The oak tree has already been here and told me the truth."

"What do you mean?" the other man said, "No tree came here. I've been here with you the whole time."

"How did you know that he had not reached the oak tree when I asked you?" the judge asked. "And how did you know that he had reached the oak tree when I asked you again later? Surely you were in the forest and you knew where the tree was. Surely you took the gold coins from this man. Now you will return the one hundred gold pieces and also pay a fine for trying to cheat him."

So, the tree was a witness without leaving the forest and justice was done.

A Test of Friendship

A Nigerian folktale

What does "friendship" mean to you? In this folktale from Africa a wise person teaches a lesson in friendship. It is a "moralistic" folktale.

Once there were two neighbors named Olaleye and Omoteyji. They each had a small farm and they were friends. Each morning they talked and walked together to their fields.

VOCABULARY

yams a vegetable like a potato
hoe a tool used to cut weeds
irritated angry
argument fight with words
back down admit you are wrong

A wise man living nearby saw their friendship. "I think I'll test their friendship," he said. "I wonder if they are really good friends."

Secretly, the wise man made a hat for himself. He made one side of the hat red and the other side green. Then he took a walk.

"Good morning, Omoteyji!" he said, "I see you have fine yams in your field!"

"Yes," replied Omoteyji, putting his hoe down, "And I see you have a fine red hat!"

"Oh, yes!" the wise man said, "I am happy you noticed it." The wise man continued his walk and Omoteyji continued his work.

Soon the wise man saw Olaleye.

"Good morning, Olaleye!" he called, "I see you have fine yams in your field!"

"Yes," replied Olaleye, putting his hoe down, "And I see you have a fine green hat!"

"Oh, yes!" the wise man said, "I am happy you noticed it. I looked a long time before I found the one I wanted."

Soon it was noon. Olaleye and Omoteyji sat down for lunch together.

"Did you see that fine red hat our neighbor was wearing this morning?" Omoteyji asked.

Olaleye laughed. "You must have been weakened by the sun, my friend. What red hat? He was wearing a green hat."

"A green hat? Oh, no," Omoteyji said, irritated. "You were the one weakened by the sun, my friend. I know his hat was red."

The men had a terrible argument. Neither man would back down. Each man insisted he was right. Soon they came to blows.

"What's this?" the wise man said, running up to them. "You two fighting! I thought you were the best of friends! How can friends come to blows like this?"

Olaleye and Omoteyji cooled down. Then they saw the hat once again on the wise man's head. But this time Omoteyji saw the green side and Olaleye saw the red side.

"Omoteyji, my friend," Olaleye said quickly, "You were right. The hat is red."

"Oh, no," Omoteyji said, "I was the one weakened by the sun. The hat is green."

Once again the men argued. The argument got hotter and hotter until the two men were about to come to blows. Then the wise man laughed and took his hat off.

"Look," he said. "The hat is green on one side and red on the other. You were both right. But you were both wrong about your friendship. You are not good friends if you cannot examine both sides of a question without anger."

Omoteyji and Olaleye understood the wise man. They laughed and returned to their yams and became stronger friends than ever.

Little Burnt-Face

An Apache folktale

In this folktale, the woman named Little Burnt-Face is the face of the desert during the hot summer. The great chief is the rain. The symbol of the rain is the rainbow. The rain is invisible during dry weather, but then returns at last and restores beauty to the burnt face of the earth.

Long ago there was a village on a lake. One family in the village had three daughters. The two older daughters were cruel to their younger sister. She was beautiful and they were jealous.

One day their father was hunting. Their mother was busy by the lake. The older sisters took hot coals from the fire and burned the face of their younger sister. When their father returned, he asked. "What happened while I was gone?"

"She fell in the fire," the older sisters said. "She disobeyed us and went near the fire. She's not good for anything."

The father scolded his youngest daughter and she left, crying. From that day on, everyone in the village called her Little Burnt-Face.

At the edge of the village, near the lake, there was a beautiful teepee. A great chief lived there with his sister. The great chief was invisible. No one had ever seen him except his sister. When people visited him, all they saw were his moccasins.

One spring his sister said, "The great chief will marry any girl who can see him." All the girls in the village visited the sister. The sister took them to the lake and asked each one, "Do you see my brother?"

VOCABULARY

scolded   disciplined with words
teepee   a Native American
   home
invisible   cannot be seen
moccasins   Native American
   shoes
lashings   rope

"Yes," they said, as they walked by the water.

"Describe his shoulder strap," the sister said.

"It is a strip of rawhide," the girls replied.

"How does he pull his dog sled?" the sister asked.

"With green lashings," the girls replied.

Then the sister knew that no one had seen her brother and she told them all to go home.

Finally only three girls hadn't spoken to the sister. The girls were Little Burnt-Face and her two sisters. The two older sisters dressed in their best clothes and left for the teepee. Little Burnt-Face followed. Everyone laughed at her because her face was burned and her hair was burned off and her clothes were ugly.

The great chief's sister, however, was kind and asked Little Burnt-Face to stay. They left the teepee and walked by the lake.

"Do you see my brother?" she asked the two older sisters.

"Yes," the older sisters said.

"Describe his shoulder strap."

"It is a strip of rawhide."

"And how does he pull his dog sled?"

"With green lashings."

Then the sister turned to Little Burnt-Face and asked. "Do you see my brother?"

"Yes, I do," Little Burnt-Face said. "He is wonderful."

"How does he pull his dog sled?" the sister asked.

"With a beautiful rainbow," Little Burnt-Face replied.

"And what is his bow-string made of?"

"It is made of the Milky Way," Little Burnt-Face replied.

The great chief's sister smiled with joy and took the hand of Little Burnt-Face.

"You have surely seen my brother," she said.

She took Little Burnt-Face back to the teepee of the great chief. Then she washed Little Burnt-Face with dew until her burns disappeared and her skin was soft and beautiful. Little Burnt-Face's hair grew long again and dark like the Blackbird's wing. Then the great chief's sister dressed Little Burnt-Face in a beautiful wedding gown.

The great chief appeared. He was no longer invisible. He saw his beautiful bride and he whispered, "We have finally found each other."

"Yes," Little Burnt-Face said.

There was a great celebration. It lasted for days. All the people of the village came, except the two older sisters. They crept back to their house weeping in shame.

The Banza

A Haitian folktale

Do you have a "lucky charm" in your culture? Something that will protect you or bring you good luck? This folktale, from the island of Haiti in the Caribbean Sea, is about a lucky charm. It is a "trickery" folktale.

Once on the island of Haiti there lived a small tiger named Teegra and a small goat named Cabree. Usually tigers and goats are enemies, but Teegra and Cabree were friends.

One day they were playing in the forest and they got lost. Suddenly three big tigers appeared.

"Mama! Papa! Auntie!" Teegra cried with joy and Teegra left Cabree and followed them home. The next day Teegra remembered Cabree and visited her in the forest.

"I brought you a banza," Teegra said.

"What's a banza?" Cabree asked.

"It's a small banjo," Teegra said. "Hold it over your heart and it will protect you."

Teegra went back home.

Cabree looked at the beautiful banza. She played the strings and the music was wonderful.

VOCABULARY

menacingly   threateningly
ferocious   mean

One day four large tigers found Cabree. They were hungry and wanted to eat her. Six more tigers appeared and now there were ten.

"What's that around your neck?" the lead tiger asked menacingly. Cabree was frightened and reached for her heart. Her hand hit the banza and the strings played music.

The leader of the tigers laughed. "Oh, so you want to play us a song?"

"No," said Cabree. All the tigers were angry and moved closer. "Well, all right," Cabree said. Cabree played the banza and started to sing. To her great surprise, her voice was low and ferocious:

> Ten fat tigers, ten fat tigers.
> Cabree eats tigers raw.
> Yesterday Cabree ate ten tigers.
> Today Cabree eats ten more.

The tigers were afraid.

"Who is Cabree?" one tiger asked.

"I am Cabree," Cabree said in a ferocious voice that scared even her. "And I always sing before dinner." Five tigers ran away.

Cabree stared at the other five. Then she sang again in a ferocious voice:

> Five fat tigers, five fat tigers.
> Cabree eats tigers raw.
> Yesterday Cabree ate ten tigers.
> Today Cabree eats five more.

Four tigers ran away. Now only the lead tiger remained.

"One fat tiger, one fat tiger," Cabree sang in her ferocious voice, but the tiger stopped her.

"Please," the tiger said. "Let me go. I promise you no tiger will ever bother you again."

"All right, I'll let you go," Cabree said. "But you must do one thing for me. Find the little tiger named Teegra. Tell Teegra that today Cabree's heart and the banza are one."

And so it was. The banza had protected Cabree from the tigers.

How the Tiger Got Its Stripes

A Vietnamese folktale

The Vietnamese were ruled by China for 1,000 years. Then they were ruled by the French for 200 years. Their folktales are often stories about weaker people outwitting stronger people. This is an "origin" folktale.

A long time ago tigers didn't have stripes. They were one solid color. One day a brown tiger wandered into a rice field looking for food. He saw a huge water buffalo pulling a plow for a tiny man. Each time the farmer whipped the water buffalo on its back, the water buffalo pulled even harder.

The tiger watched the water buffalo straining and pulling and suffering. The tiger grew hungrier and the water buffalo looked more delicious. Finally the tiger said to the water buffalo, "Why does a powerful animal like you allow a small, weak man like him to make you suffer? You could pick him up and eat him just as easily as I can eat you."

VOCABULARY

wandered walked
water buffalo a huge animal used in the field
straining working very hard
delicious very good to eat
powerful very strong

"This small man has the intelligence to make me work," the buffalo said. "That's why I let him do this."

"Intelligence?" the tiger asked. "What is intelligence?"

"I don't know, because I don't have it," the water buffalo answered. "Ask the man."

The tiger was proud of being the most feared animal in the jungle, but he had never heard of intelligence. He looked at the small skinny farmer and the huge water buffalo.

Intelligence makes it possible for the man to control that huge animal, the tiger thought. Think what I could do with intelligence! I would never have to worry about my next meal.

The tiger approached the man. "What is intelligence?" he asked the man. "I want to see it."

"I can explain what it is, but I cannot show it to you," the man said. "I left it at home. But if I go home to get it, you will eat my water buffalo."

"I will not eat your water buffalo," the tiger said. "I promise."

"I do not trust you," the man said. "As soon as I turn my back, you will eat my water buffalo."

"Then what can I do to convince you that I won't?" the tiger asked.

"Let me tie you to that tree while I go home to get my intelligence. When I come back I will untie you."

The tiger agreed and lay down by the tree. The man scratched his head and said, "I can't tie you if you lie down."

"Do you want me to sit up?" the tiger asked.

"Yes," the farmer said. "Good. That's better. Now put your four legs around the tree."

The farmer tied the tiger firmly to the tree. Then he left and returned with an armful of dry grass. He put the grass underneath the tiger. He picked up his whip and beat the tiger. "This is my intelligence," he said, "and since you're so stupid, I will burn you and eat you."

The farmer set the grass on fire. When the flames reached the tiger they burnt the rope that held the tiger to the tree. The tiger roared in pain. Then he broke free and ran away.

Ever since then, tigers have dark stripes from the burn marks left by the scorched rope.

The Coyote Rings the Wrong Bell

A Mexican folktale

In this folktale a rabbit outwits a hungry coyote. It is a "trickery" folktale.

One day Señor Rabbit took a siesta. He went to sleep under a big tree. Señor Coyote walked by. He was hungry. Señor Coyote hadn't eaten for days. So he walked up to the tree and grabbed the rabbit.

"Ah, ha!" said Señor Coyote. "I've got you!"

Señor Rabbit was frightened.

"Mmmm," said the coyote. "You feel nice and fat. You'll make a good lunch for me."

The rabbit was smart and thought of a plan.

VOCABULARY

coyote   a small wolf
siesta   a nap

"I'm very old," the rabbit said. "My meat is dry and tough. I don't mind if you eat me. I'm going to die soon. But do me one last favor."

"What favor?" the coyote asked.

"I have to ring the school bell for all the juicy little rabbits in the schoolhouse over there."

"Did you say, 'juicy little rabbits?'"

"Oh, yes. Juicy and tender."

"Where is the bell?" the coyote asked.

Señor Rabbit pointed to a hornet's nest in a tree. "There it is," he said. "I shake the tree very hard and the bell rings."

"And the juicy little rabbits come out?"

"Every time."

"Well, I don't think I will eat you," said Señor Coyote. "Why don't you go for a little walk? I'll ring the bell for you."

"No, I must do it myself," the rabbit said. "It's a very important job."

"Oh, please let me do it," the coyote said. "I want to do you a favor."

"Well, if you insist. But you must wait for the right time. The sun has to reach the top of the trees."

"Oh, I promise," the coyote said.

"And be sure to shake the tree hard. Otherwise, the juicy little rabbits won't hear the bell."

"Yes, I promise," the coyote said. "I'll shake it hard."

Señor Rabbit hopped away. He was laughing to himself.

When the rabbit was out of sight, Señor Coyote shook the tree hard. The hornet's nest fell on his head. The air filled with hundreds of angry hornets. They stung the coyote all over his body.

The coyote ran to a pond and jumped in the water. He was covered with stings. The hornets flew away. Señor Coyote stepped out of the pond and looked at his reflection in the water.

"Ouch!" he cried, looking at the stingers in his body. "I look like a porcupine! I wanted juicy little rabbits, not porcupine hairs!"

Responding to Reading

Sharing Ideas

1. Folktales are brief stories, seldom written down, that are passed from generation to generation. Some folktales teach a lesson about life (moralistic folktales). Some folktales describe how things in nature first started (origin folktales). Some folktales tell about tricks the main characters play on each other (trickery folktales).

- ▲ Form six teams. Each team chooses one folktale from this section to read. Discuss: What lesson about life is taught in each of these folktales? Share your team's observations with the whole class.
- ▲ Discuss the difference between origin, moralistic, and trickery folktales. Can you think of examples of each from your own culture?

2. Sit with a friend or in a group. Choose one folktale and discuss how the folktale reflects its culture. Consider the animals, the food, the language, the people, the clothes, the climate, and the lesson that was taught.

3. Discuss examples of folktales from your culture. Perhaps you can sit with someone who speaks your own language. Do you have a favorite folktale? Why are these folktales important to your culture? What lessons do they teach?

4. Talk to your parents and relatives. What folktales do they remember from your culture? Do they have favorites? Who taught them the folktales? Why are they special to your culture? What lessons do they teach? Share them with the class.

5. After discussing folktales from different cultures, did you find any folktales that are similar? How is the same folktale expressed through different cultures?

6. Why are folktales such a powerful way to teach lessons about life? Consider the fact that some cultures do not, or did not, have a writing system.

7. Share other things from your culture with your class. Consider folk art, dance, songs, and traditions. Do any folktales from your culture reflect these other art forms?

Writing About Folktales

1. Rewrite the ending to any of these folktales. How would you change the ending? Why?

2. Adapt any of these folktales to your own culture. Which words would you change? Why? What information would you remove? Why? What information would you add? Why?

3. Make a list of the lessons about life that you want to pass on to your children. If possible, write each lesson in a simple sentence. For example, "Respect your parents," or "Always tell the truth." What values are important to you? Why?

4. Write a folktale. Remember a folktale is a simple story. It usually teaches a lesson about life. Animals often talk. It may be an origin, moralistic, or trickery folktale. You may want to "brainstorm" on ideas first. You may want to write an outline before you start writing.

5. Rewrite one of the folktales as a play. Write dialogue and stage directions. Perform the play for other students.

More Reading

Living Tapestries, Folk Tales of the Hmong, Charles H. Numrich. Fairway Press, 1985.

Cambodian Folk Tales from the Gatiloke, Carrison and Chhean. Charles E. Tuttle Company, 1987.

Under the Starfruit Tree, Folktales from Vietnam, Alice Terada. A Kolowalu Book, University of Hawaii Press, 1989.

Kalila and Dimnah: Fables From the Middle East, Hassan Tehranchian. Outlet Books, 1985.

Folktales of Mexico, Americo Paredes. University of Chicago Press, 1970.

African Tales: Folklore of the Central African Republic, translated by Polly Strong. Tell Publications, 1992.

The Woe Shirt: Caribbean Folktales, Paule Barton. Graywolf Press, 1982.

The Talking Stone, An Anthology of Native American Tales and Legends, Dorothy de Wit. Greenwillow Books, 1979.

Ukrainian Folktales, Marie Bloch. Coward/McCann, 1964.

The Day It Snowed Tortillas, Joe Hayes. Mariposa Publishing, 1982.

My Grandmother's Stories: A Collection of Jewish Folk Tales, Adele Geras. Alfred A. Knopf/Borzoi Sprinters, 1990.

The Sound of Flutes and Other Indian Legends, Lame Dear, Jenny Leading Cloud, and Leonard Crow Dog. Pantheon Books, 1976.

Land of the Long White Cloud: Maori Myths, Tales, and Legends, Kiri Te Kanawa. Arcade, 1990.

The People Could Fly: American Black Folktales, Virginia Hamilton. Alfred A. Knopf, 1985.

Tales of Triumph

Out of poverty, poetry.
Out of misery, song.

A Mexican saying

The Undefeated

An immigrant boy gets lost in the world of gangs and drugs. Can he be saved? Maybe. But not without a struggle.

Part 1

Eddie Ramirez closed his eyes. He didn't want to see the pain in his life anymore. He tried to run, but he couldn't run fast enough to escape the voices inside his skull.

"Don't do it, Eddie," he heard his father say.

"Stop, Eddie," he heard his mother say.

"Where are you, Eddie?" he heard his brother say.

"Come back, Eddie," he heard his track coach say.

"Remember me, Eddie?" he heard his girlfriend say.

Why didn't everyone leave him alone? He put his hands to his head and ran and ran down the hot streets of Los Angeles, into the night, into the day, always running...away from school, away from his family, away from his track coach, away from his girlfriend, away from everything...away, away and into the world of gangs and drugs.

The gang gave Eddie a new family. The drugs gave Eddie money. The drugs made him feel better, too. They took away the anger that burned in him every day like hot concrete, the anger toward everybody and everything. The drugs took away the despair he felt when he thought the good life in the United States would never be his.

The American dream was an illusion, wasn't it? It was some cruel joke played on immigrants, right? Come to the United States and make it, right? Start your new life in the land of opportunity,

VOCABULARY

skull   head
despair   without hope
poverty   without money

right? Work hard, study hard, get a good education and the dream will be yours, right? A nice house, a nice car, lots of money.

But that wasn't Eddie's world. Eddie's world was poverty. His friends lived in cheap houses with leaky plumbing and holes in the walls. His father stepped on cockroaches when he got up at night to go to work on an assembly line. So one day Eddie Ramirez gave it all up. He quit school and joined a gang and turned to drugs.

Gang life was violent. They robbed. They beat people. They stole cars. They shot at the police. They drank alcohol. They sold drugs. And they died. One by one, Eddie Ramirez saw his new friends die, either shot by the police or shot by rival gangs.

Part 2

That would have been the end of Eddie's life, too, except one night he got drunk and smashed his car. It was a terrible accident. Eddie was driving too fast and struck a telephone pole. He hit his head and then he went unconscious.

Somewhere in the dream world that followed, Eddie Ramirez heard the voices again. He didn't know if he was alive or dead. He didn't know if he was dreaming or awake. He didn't know where he was, unaware that he was in the emergency room of a hospital.

VOCABULARY

struck hit
wheel him out push him out
consumed him taken over his life
craving strong need for

"Eddie," he heard his mother say, "Come home, son." Her voice was full of love for him. His father was there, too, and his brother and his track coach and his girlfriend. They were all talking to him, somewhere inside his head, or was it outside his head now? He didn't know because he didn't know where he was or what had happened. Then he heard another voice, like someone talking through water. "Wheel him out. He's going to live."

For the next few weeks Eddie Ramirez lived in two worlds. There was the dream world of sleep and there was the awake world of his hospital room. For a few moments every day he woke up and tried to move his crushed body. There was only pain in that world as the blood and bones and skin of his broken body struggled to heal itself.

Most of the time he slept in the dream world. Eddie lived in the dream world for a long time. In the dream world all hatred was gone. There was no anger anymore. There was no despair. There was only rest and the voices of people who loved him. The voices spoke to him every day and Eddie listened. He had gotten lost in his own hatred. He had shut out people who still loved him. The pain in his life had consumed him and now he had to face it.

When Eddie woke up for good from the accident he was different. His anger and hatred toward everybody was gone. It was as if the accident had crushed it all out of his body. He wanted his life to be different now. He quit the gang and started school again. He thought about ways to succeed, not ways to fail. He didn't hate America anymore, either. He thought about the millions of new people who had just come to the United States and he wanted them to succeed, too. Many had waited years to come. Many would have died in their own country had they stayed. Many had no place else to go.

Eddie talked to his track coach and started training again, but his struggle wasn't over. He had become addicted to cocaine while he was in the gang and he was helpless against the craving. He knew he needed help.

Part 3

Eddie left school for ten weeks and entered a drug rehabilitation center. In the center he told his story to people just like himself and they listened quietly. Nobody judged him. Nobody shamed him. Nobody said he was a bad person. They understood the craving for drugs because they had it. They understood the helpless feeling of the craving taking over their lives.

Eddie stayed at the center and when he shook and sweated and threatened to run away, the others helped him and kept his life going forward toward rehabilitation, not backward toward destruction again.

But rehabilitation was hard. The car accident was easy compared to this. The accident was pain to just his bones and blood

VOCABULARY

drug rehabilitation center
drug treatment center
overwhelmed   overcame

and skin, but cocaine addiction was pain to his soul. Many times Eddie wondered if he would ever heal.

"You only have to be drug-free for today, Eddie," his counselor said, "not for the rest of your life. Rehabilitation is one day at a time."

Eddie Ramirez was determined. He went through the program, but he went too fast. He thought he was cured, but he wasn't. One night when the craving for cocaine overwhelmed him, he ran away. He visited his old friends on the streets of Los Angeles. He bought some cocaine and took it and the old feeling of power came back. His body suddenly felt strong again, not weak and broken from the car accident. But then he ran out of money and his old friends wouldn't talk to him anymore.

He called the rehabilitation center.

"This is Eddie Ramirez," he said. "I need help."

"Eddie, where are you?" someone said and Eddie gave them an address. In a short time his friends found him, shaking and scared, and they brought him back to the center. Nobody judged him in the car. Nobody shamed him. They all had been rescued themselves.

Part 4

When Eddie returned to the center, his counselor spoke to him again. "The addiction is bigger than you, Eddie," his counselor said. "Remember the first step of the program."

Eddie Ramirez started all over again. He didn't give up. He read the first step again. "We admit we are powerless over drugs, that our lives have become unmanageable." Yes, the addiction was bigger than he was. He may have it all his life. But there was help and he was determined to make it.

VOCABULARY

unmanageable out of control
courteous kind
criticize say negative words
  about someone

Eddie Ramirez read the program guidebook every day. He took notes now and his life continued to change. This time he hoped it was for good. Each day he wrote little reminders to himself.

"Just for today I will be unafraid."

"Just for today I will have a program."

"Just for today I will be courteous and not criticize others."

His counselor was happy. "That's it, Eddie," he said, "One day at a time."

And that's how Eddie lived now, one drug-free day at a time. The past was dead. The future wasn't here yet. He was alive now, in the present moment. Was he drug-free today or not?

Part 5

Soon the time came for Eddie Ramirez to leave the rehabilitation center.

"We want you to help in your school, Eddie," his counselor said. "Will you talk to the other kids?"

Eddie agreed.

The first time he spoke he was afraid. "Just for today I will be unafraid," he told himself as he spoke to the group. They were his own age. Would they laugh at him? No, they listened and asked questions and he spoke about the craving for cocaine and how it never goes away.

Then one night he got a telephone call. He was living with his parents again and his mom called him to the phone.

"Who is it, Eddie?" she asked. "It's so late. You've got school to-morrow, honey."

"I know, Mom," Eddie said. "I won't be long. I promise."

Eddie picked up the phone. "Hello?" he said.

"Eddie Ramirez?"

"Yes."

"I heard you talk in school today. I need help."

Eddie wrote down the boy's name. Then he tried to talk to him. The boy was scared.

"Where are you?" Eddie asked.

"Downtown. On the street," the boy said. Eddie wrote down the address.

"I have to go, Mom," he said, "I'll call you as soon as I can."

"It's not your old friends, is it Eddie?"

"No, it's somebody from school."

A little while later Eddie found a young boy suffering from cocaine addiction. The boy was shaking and scared. He was full of anger and hatred toward everybody and everything. He hated school. He hated the police. He hated his parents. He hated himself.

Eddie looked into the boy's eyes and understood the anger. "I can help you," Eddie said. "But you have to want the help. It won't be easy." There was no judgment in his voice, no shame.

"All right," the boy said. Eddie helped the boy to his car. It was night and they drove down the dark streets of Los Angeles. Eddie remembered the old days, when he loved the street and the world of gangs and drugs and fast cars, but that was behind him now. There was no satisfaction in that world, only darkness and death.

Eddie drove to the drug rehabilitation center. He explained the purpose of the center carefully to the boy. He told him the program was difficult, but they would help him.

"Do you want to go in?" Eddie asked.

"Yes," the boy said.

The two of them got out. Eddie put his arm around the boy's shoulder and together they walked into the building.

The Girl from Kiev

Even in Ukraine, Rada Kalinka was a shy girl. Now it was worse. She was new to the United States and still so very shy. How would she ever make friends? In this story, she uses a special talent to adjust to her new life.

Part 1

When Rada Kalinka first started school in the United States she was terrified. She was so shy, so terribly shy.

"Now, now, Rada," her mother said. "You will learn English soon and then it will be easier." But English was hard. Each day Rada struggled and struggled. Many nights she cried.

"It's because you're so shy," her mother said. "You can't be shy, Rada. You must speak up in school."

But that was impossible. She was in a new country. She didn't speak the language. She didn't have any friends. Every day was a terrible, lonely struggle and she was losing the struggle, too. She was withdrawing more and more, afraid to speak to anyone.

Well, almost anyone. There was one person who understood her. That person was Mrs. Benson, the ESL teacher. Rada loved her class. Mrs. Benson had a wonderful smile. The smile said, "I understand your struggle, Rada. I'm here to help you." Mrs. Benson told her that every day without speaking a word of English. She told her with her smile.

Slowly Rada started to speak English. Sometimes she stayed after school just to be with Mrs. Benson. Rada needed a smile, a friendly face, encouragement, a gentle voice, and Mrs. Benson understood.

One day Mrs. Benson showed everyone pictures of Kiev. Rada was proud of her home. That was where her friends lived, where

VOCABULARY

shy   afraid to speak; soft-spoken
withdrawing   not speaking to anyone
ESL   English as a Second Language
skipped   did not go to class
hobby   something you like to do

her grandmother lived, and where she used to walk to school. And nobody laughed at the pictures because Mrs. Benson talked about respect.

"We must respect other cultures," Mrs. Benson said. "In this class your old life and your new life come together in a respectful way." Rada understood. Respect meant no one should laugh at someone else for being different.

Then one day Mrs. Benson said, "Tomorrow is hobby day. I want each of you to bring in your favorite hobby and talk about it."

"Hobby?" someone asked.

"Yes," Mrs. Benson said, "Goldfish, stamps, drawing, baseball cards. Something you like to do, or play, or save."

Rada smiled.

That night at home she took out a box. The box was made of hand-carved wood. It was a family treasure and her favorite hobby was inside.

"Can I take this to school tomorrow, mother?" she said.

"Of course, dear," her mother said, sitting down next to her, "And if anyone beats you in that game, bring them home and I'll make them a bowl of my best soup!"

Rada laughed.

"It's so good to hear you laugh again, dear," her mother said, putting her arm around her. "I've been so worried about you. I know it's hard, Rada. But there's nothing for us back home. Nothing, not even enough to eat. Many people are waiting to come here. We are the lucky ones. Soon something good will happen to you and everything will be all right. Trust me."

Rada's mother kissed her and held her for a moment. A tear from her mother's face splashed on Rada's hand. "Trust me," her mother whispered. "Something good will happen soon."

Part 2

The next morning Rada counted the beautiful wooden pieces in the box. They were all there. She was excited for the first time about going to school.

"Today is hobby day," Mrs. Benson said. "I want each person to talk about their favorite hobby. Who would like to be first?"

"These birds are from Haiti," a boy said, holding up pictures of colorful birds. No one in the class had ever seen birds like that before. They had long feathers and were beautiful. "I cut out their pictures and put them in this book."

"These coins are from China," a girl said. "My uncle gave them to me. Some are very old. I promised my uncle I would never sell them."

"These stamps are from the Dominican Republic," a boy said. "They tell the history of my country. These stamps are my favorite history book."

Then Rada opened her wooden box. "My hobby is chess," she said. "My grandfather was a champion in Ukraine. He taught my father and my father taught me. I was our school champion."

The other students looked at the carved wooden pieces.

"Who made these pieces?" a boy asked.

"A man back home," Rada replied. "Each piece is hand carved."

"Will you teach us how to play?" another student asked.

"Yes," Rada said. Mrs. Benson nodded and Rada set up the chess board. She did it with ease. The chess pieces were almost part of her fingers. Then she held up the pieces one by one.

"That's a pawn," Mrs. Benson said, helping with the English. "And that's a rook, and a knight, and a bishop, and the King and the Queen."

Rada showed the others how to move the pieces. They liked the game. Soon she and her new friends started to play chess every day in school. Sometimes they played during ESL class. Sometimes they played during lunch hour.

One day during lunch hour Rada was playing four students at the same time. A crowd of students had gathered around. Rada went from board to board, moving her pieces with total confidence, hardly pausing to think. The students watching were amazed. So was the principal. The next day he started a chess club in school and he asked Rada to be the teacher.

"This is how you start a game," Rada said. There were lots of students who wanted to learn. She showed them some of the opening moves her father had taught her.

A few days later she said, "Now we will practice the middle game," and she explained the variety of moves possible in the middle game.

A few days later she said, "Now we will practice the end game," and she explained the variety of moves in the end game. "The important thing is to capture the King. Then you win. You say 'checkmate' and the game is over."

Part 3

One day the principal planned a chess tournament. Sixty-four students signed up to play. The students played every day during lunch hour for five days. Hundreds of other students watched. After one round, 32 players were left. After two rounds, 16 players were left. After three rounds, eight players were left. After four rounds, four players were left. After five rounds, only two players were left, Rada and a boy named Sam Taylor.

VOCABULARY

tournament   contest
round   one game
countered   moved
aggressive   strong; forceful
castled   protected the King
thrust   forceful move
relentlessly   without giving up

The championship game was set for the next day. Someone made a big sign that said: CHESS CHAMPIONSHIP TODAY! RADA VERSUS SAM! TODAY! DURING LUNCH HOUR!

Hundreds of students came to watch. Rada sat down at a table. Sam Taylor sat across from her. He was a quiet boy with kind eyes and Rada wondered about him. How good was he at chess? She soon found out.

Sam Taylor picked white and moved first. He moved his King pawn two spaces forward. It was a strong, bold move. Rada countered with her Queen bishop pawn. Sam Taylor smiled, just slightly, as if to say, "the Sicilian Defense," and Rada knew this boy could play.

Sam Taylor moved his knight. Rada countered. Sam moved again and Rada countered. Each move Sam made was strong and bold and he attacked and captured the center of the board.

Rada wondered again about this quiet boy. He was so quiet, but his chess game was so aggressive. His game was opposite from his outer personality and Rada remembered her father's words: "You never know someone until you play them in chess, Rada."

The game proceeded to the middle game. Sam still had the offensive. He had developed his pieces beautifully and Rada had countered perfectly. The game was even. Both of them had castled. Rada knew that Sam had a decision to make. He had to continue to attack and trade pieces, or play conservative and protect his King. What would he do?

With no hesitation, Sam Taylor struck again. He advanced a bishop and fearlessly traded pieces. Rada thought of her father again: "Let the bold players hang themselves, Rada. Set a trap."

Sam Taylor tried to break Rada's defense. He struck again and again but Rada traded pieces and kept her King well protected. Then she set the trap. She gave Sam a free pawn and he took it. He took it too quickly and Rada countered with her Queen. It was a strong thrust, seemingly out of nowhere, that suddenly gave her the offensive. Sam Taylor saw his mistake, but it was too late. Rada pushed her pieces now, driving relentlessly toward his King. Her moves were perfect.

"Check," she said, but Sam moved out of it.

"Check," she said again, but Sam moved away again.

Then Rada captured a rook and two pawns and Sam's game fell apart.

"Checkmate," she finally said and the game ended.

Sam Taylor looked at Rada. He put his hand out and smiled. Rada shook his hand and smiled back. Sam's face was kind, even in defeat, and Rada knew she had a new friend. The crowd cheered. The crowd! Rada thought. She had forgotten about the crowd. They cheered for her and then they walked over and congratulated her.

Two weeks later Rada Kalinka received an award during a school assembly. There was no fear in her steps now as she walked up in front of her new friends to receive her award. There was no fear in her voice as she spoke a few words, in English, to the entire school.

Rada sat down. Her mother was right, she thought. Something good did happen to her, but it was more than just winning a chess game. She wasn't shy anymore. Today when she stood up in front of everyone she looked fear in the face for the final time and she won that game, too.

"Checkmate," she whispered, laughing to herself and loving her new home.

Margarita's World

Margarita García was from Puerto Rico. She was young, beautiful, and handicapped. Other people might have felt sorry for themselves, but Margarita just laughed. "What good is it if your legs are alive but your heart is dead?" she said. In this story, she shares her heart with someone special.

Part 1

It was a beautiful summer afternoon in New York City. The sky was warm and clear. Margarita García pushed her wheelchair down a sunny path in the Central Park Zoo.

"Slow down, Margarita!" her older sister called. "You're going too fast!"

"Nonsense!" Margarita said, laughing. "You're such a worry-wart."

When they came to the sea lions, Margarita stopped. Her sister caught up and put her arm around Margarita's shoulder. "Are you sure you'll be all right here, Margarita?"

"Of course," Margarita answered. "Go. Good-bye. Scram. Go meet Julio. I'll be fine. You'll be back for the concert, right?"

"In two hours, Margarita. It starts at four. We'll meet you right here, in front of the sea lions, okay? There's a police officer over there if you need anything."

"Yes, yes. I'll be fine. Good-bye. Go. *Hasta luego. Hasta la vista. Hasta la próxima.*"

They both laughed.

"And don't be late!" Margarita called. "I want to sit right next to the stage!" Margarita watched her sister disappear into the summer crowd. Then she pushed herself close to the sea lions and took out her sketchbook.

Now let me see, she said to herself, looking at the sea lions through the eyes of an artist. Their bodies are incredibly smooth. They have whiskered faces. They swim in a circular pool filled with greenish water and they are always barking for food.

Margarita drew quickly. She was a beautiful artist. Oh, yes, she thought, and they love that cement island. And look at all those pigeons eating popcorn and peanuts just inside the cage. You would think they hadn't eaten for weeks. And maybe, just maybe, I can get those huge, straight, cream-colored buildings far off on the skyline, just like that. Perfect!

When she finished her close-up sketches she pushed her wheelchair under a tree and drew pictures from a distance. There's the polar bear cage, she said to herself. And look at that restaurant over there with the lovely red and white awning. And that huge stone eagle over there by the steps. And what are those things on the corners of the pool? They look like four oriental wire cages trimmed with gold.

The pages in her sketchbook filled quickly. Under each drawing she wrote the date and the location. Finally she closed her book and bought popcorn and a soft drink. Then she sat in the beautiful afternoon sunshine and watched people.

VOCABULARY

worrywart someone who worries too much

scram go away

hasta luego "see you later" in Spanish

hasta la vista "so long" in Spanish

hasta la próxima "see you again" in Spanish

sketchbook a book for drawing

awning protects a window from sunlight

Part 2

There were so many people coming and going. They were so busy, too.

"Oh, Oliver, come here!" a mother said, picking up her small boy and brushing dirt off his clothes. Margarita laughed.

"Did you catch that article in *Time* magazine last week, Dave?" a man in a suit said.

"The next time you're in San Francisco, Amy, you have to visit City Lights bookstore," a woman said. "It used to be Ferlinghetti's place." Margarita could smell her patchouli oil.

"Excuse me, officer," a tourist said. "Do you know what kind of trees those are?"

"I have no idea," the police officer said, adjusting his blue helmet.

Then a whole group of children came. They ran screaming toward the sea lions.

"Come here, seal!"

"Here, seal, seal, seal!"

"Not much of a tail!"

"They sound like dogs!"

"I want to go to the zoo!"

"You're in the zoo!"

"Look at that one!"

"Should I give him my sandwich?"

"Hey, you, seal!"

"I want all the boys over here!" a man yelled. "Now!"

"Rosemary, get the girls!" a woman yelled. "We're leaving." An old man sneezed and all the children laughed. Then it was quiet again.

The sun was warm on Margarita's face. Church bells chimed in the distance. The air was full of pigeons. A police officer rode by on a horse. Margarita waved and he waved back. Then she looked at her watch. Oh, no! she said to herself. Only another half an hour.

She pushed her wheelchair over to a band shell surrounded by green benches and drew pictures. Then she drew pictures of the

VOCABULARY

article story
Ferlinghetti an American poet
patchouli oil perfume
chimed rang
band shell outdoor concert area
José Feliciano a blind Puerto Rican singer

huge statues and wrote down their names: Fitz Green Halleck. Beethoven. Johann Christoph Friedrich von Shiller. Robert Burns. Walter Scott.

"Margarita?" someone called from a distance. It was her sister.

"Over here!" Margarita answered.

Her sister walked over. She was alone and looked sad.

"Where's Julio?" Margarita asked.

"He's being a jerk."

"Isn't he coming to the concert?"

"No. We broke up. What a total jerk." Then her sister started crying. Margarita took her hand.

"He wasn't worth it," Margarita said. "Come on. Let's go to the concert. You'll feel better."

"Can I push you?"

"Of course not."

Margarita pushed her wheelchair into a crowd of young people. They were all walking to the concert. José Feliciano was giving a free concert in a huge meadow in the park. Margarita pushed closer until she got next to the stage. There was a special section for people in wheelchairs.

When the concert started, José Feliciano came on the stage. Someone helped him because he was blind. He sat down and played his guitar beautifully and Margarita was touched. How did you learn to play like that? she thought. You're blind. And how did you learn to sing like that? You can't see the notes. Your voice is so loving and your face is so gentle and you sing free for us. I wish I could be your eyes so you could see the sky and the clouds and the beautiful stars at night, so you could see the birds that you hear and the flowers that you smell. Your voice is so strong and free. Yes, your eyes are dead, but your heart is alive.

"What beautiful songs," Margarita whispered. "I'm so glad we came."

Margarita looked up toward the sky. Sea gulls floated like feathers in the air. The clouds were lovely. Her thoughts came and went like the beautiful clouds and she thought of all the things she wanted to do with her life, all the pictures she wanted to paint, all the places she wanted to visit, all the people she wanted to meet. How would she ever find the time?

Through the late afternoon breeze, scented with summer, she heard the strong, free voice of José Feliciano again and her heart was open like his and it was wonderful. Her dead legs didn't matter. His dead eyes didn't matter. His beautiful songs were filled with joy and compassion. Somehow love and courage had survived in his life when they could have easily died with his eyes. Margarita put her head back and looked toward the beautiful sky and she was happy.

A Journey to Love

The Story of Joua Yang

Many Hmong people have left Laos and come to the United States. To escape from Laos, they had to walk through the jungle and swim the Mekong River to Thailand. In Thailand they waited in refugee camps until they could go to a free country. In this true story, a young Hmong child is lost in the jungle when her family is ambushed by soldiers.

Part 1

Joua Yang was born in Laos in 1975. Her parents, Yer and Xao Yang, loved her very much and had a special ceremony called *hu plig* to celebrate her birth. However, there was a terrible war in Laos. The Hmong people were being killed for helping the United States during the Vietnam War.

VOCABULARY

ambush   surprise attack
ceremony   formal celebration

"We must leave," Xao Yang said, twelve days after tiny Joua's birth. "If we don't leave soon, we will all be killed." Xao had been a pilot and had helped the United States. Surely the soldiers would kill him. He knew it wasn't safe for his wife and new daughter, either.

Yer and Xao Yang looked at their home in Laos for the last time. Yer picked up tiny Joua, her beautiful baby, and sang to her softly. Then Yer and Xao left with a few relatives, taking only what they could carry.

The first part of the trip went fast. They got a car and drove toward Long Cheng, the headquarters of the Hmong army. The United States was airlifting Hmong people from there to safety.

But when they got close to Long Cheng, thousands of Hmong people were on the road. They were all trying desperately to reach Long Cheng and the safety of their own soldiers. Then Xao Yang heard the news. Laos had fallen, and the Hmong army was gone, evacuated out of the country. There was no safety in Long Cheng. Their only hope now was to escape to Thailand.

"Quickly," Xao Yang said, "We must leave. We can't wait here." He found a car and paid the driver. "Take us to Na Xou."

At Na Xou, the driver stopped. "I won't go any farther," he said. "It is too dangerous."

Xao and Yer Yang got out. Yer held tiny Joua close. It was night now and no one would drive them any farther. Thailand and freedom was far away. They had to walk.

"I'm sorry," Xao Yang told the others, "But Yer has just had a baby. She can't walk that far. Continue on without us. Go to Thailand and safety. We will return home until Yer is strong enough to make the trip."

The others were sad. They were afraid that Xao would be killed if he returned home. But Xao would not change his mind. Xao and Yer said good-bye to their relatives, people they had known and loved all their lives. Then they turned back.

Part 2

Xao and Yer Yang returned to their village. Some days later, there was a knock on their door.

"Are you Xao Yang?" a soldier said.

"Yes," Xao replied.

"We're from the new government. We need your help. We want to train you for a special program. Please come with us."

Xao agreed. He said good-bye to Yer and Joua and left with the soldiers. Later, Yer learned the truth. Her husband was in prison. She knew now they were all in danger, so she spoke with other relatives and Hmong villagers. Then one night, she took Joua and left with her friends and relatives to live in the jungle.

Yer Yang, Joua, and the others lived in the jungle for four years. They learned to survive. They ate what food they could. Yer refused to leave for Thailand without her husband. She waited every day for news about Xao, but news never came. Finally, after four years, a Hmong person found the group hiding in the jungle.

VOCABULARY

fawn   young deer
exhausted   tired
survivors   people who were not killed
disappeared   can not be found

105

"I will show you the way to Thailand," he said. "But we must leave now. It is through the jungle and dangerous."

Yer picked up Joua and held her close and cried softly. She knew she had to leave without Xao.

Joua was four years old now. She was too little to walk by herself so her uncle carried her on his back. The entire group, 114 people, walked at night to avoid the soldiers. There were wild animals. There was little food. Some people died.

Then one night as they walked, the soldiers found them. It was a windy, rainy night and the group didn't see the soldiers waiting to kill them. The jungle exploded in gunfire. Yer and the others screamed and ran. Half of the group, 57 people, died immediately. The rest ran for their lives. Joua clung in terror to her uncle's back. Friends and relatives, people she loved, lay dead in the grass. Then her uncle shook and fell. He had been struck by a bullet. The force of the shell jolted his body so hard that Joua fell off his back and rolled beside the tall trees. She screamed and screamed, but no one came. Then, like a tiny fawn, she lay perfectly still.

When the exhausted survivors gathered in safety, Yer realized Joua was missing.

"Joua!" she screamed, and the others covered her mouth.

"Quiet," they said, "or we will all die."

Yer struggled to break free. "I have to find Joua!" she said.

"No, no, you can't go back. She is dead. We must go on."

Yer struggled again. They held her down. They wouldn't let her up or let her cry out. She struggled and struggled until she was exhausted. The soldiers were still close by and following their tracks, so the group hid in a river. It was still raining hard. The wind blew the trees. They could see the soldiers with their rifles checking the riverbank, but they hid in the darkness.

"Joua," Yer Yang whispered that night, as the exhausted group walked on toward Thailand, "My beautiful Joua, where are you? Are you alive, or are you dead?"

Days later, Yer and the group finally reached the Mekong River. Then on a night when there was no moonlight, they swam across the river to Thailand and freedom.

Part 3

Yer Yang adjusted to life in the refugee camp. But over and over she wondered: Joua, where are you? Are you alive, or are you dead? Did you die with the others that night?

Joua Yang, just four years old, did not die with the others. She was found beside a tall tree by a kind person and taken home. Her clothes were washed and saved. Her clothes would be the only way her family could identify her if they ever came looking for her.

VOCABULARY

monastery   home of monks
orphan   child without parents

One day while Yer Yang was still in the refugee camp, she wrote her brother who was still living in Laos. Yer described the place in the jungle where Joua had been lost and asked her brother to look for her. Yer's brother received the letter and found the spot where the attack took place. Then he found a Lao couple that was raising a child who had been found in the jungle.

"These are her clothes," the Lao couple said. Yer's brother wrote a letter back to Yer in the refugee camp and described the clothes.

"Joua may be alive," Yer said. But then her brother disappeared, fearful the soldiers wanted to kill him, too.

Seven years passed. Yer Yang came to the United States. Her brother escaped to the United States, also. One day he mailed Yer a map of the place where Joua was living with the Lao couple. Yer sent the map to another relative still in Laos. This relative found the Lao family once more, but Joua was gone. She had been sent to a monastery to be raised as an orphan by monks. The relative found the monastery, but Joua was gone. She had been sent to live with a Lao woman. The relative found the Lao woman and Joua was there.

Ten years had now passed. Joua was 14. Finally, her uncle in the United States, Mr. Dao Peter Yang, was able to reach Joua by telephone.

"Joua, you're not an orphan," he said, "Your mother is here. You have a large family here. We love you."

After many delays, the necessary paperwork was completed to bring Joua Yang to the United States. The flight to Minnesota took three days. Joua was alone and scared. She could not eat or sleep. She wasn't able to speak to anyone, but each time she changed planes people pointed in the correct direction. Finally, the plane landed in Minnesota and Joua's long journey was over.

Joua Yang arrived in the United States on February 29, 1992. She was greeted by her family who had tried for ten years to find her. Now Joua lives with her mother, Yer, in St. Paul. Her father, Xao, died in a prison camp.

Responding to Reading

Sharing Ideas

1. "Triumph" means "overcome." What is the word for "triumph" in your language? We can triumph over an inner struggle, such as fear or low self-esteem, or we can triumph over an outer struggle, such as war or oppression. Discuss how each person in these stories triumphs over something. What do they overcome? Is their struggle inner or outer? Did they have help? How did their struggle and their triumph change their lives?

2. Groups of people, not just individuals, can also triumph. Discuss a group that has triumphed over something. Maybe it is a sports team. Maybe it is a group of people who worked hard for a new law. Maybe it is a group of people who overcame oppression.

3. "The Undefeated" is a story of triumph over drug addiction. Why did the boy in this story take drugs? What was the result of his addiction? How did he overcome his addiction? Do you think this story is realistic?

4. The story "The Girl From Kiev" is about overcoming fear. What fears did you face when you moved to the United States? How did you triumph over your fears?

5. Do you know someone who is handicapped? How did Margarita triumph over her handicap in the story "Margarita's World"?

6. Do you know a personal story of triumph? If you do, share it with the class. Think of your own story of struggle as a refugee or immigrant to the United States.

7. The movie *West Side Story* is about Puerto Rican immigration to the United States. Watch the movie and talk about your reaction.

Writing About Triumph

1. Write and conduct a confidential drug survey in your class or school. Consider all drugs, even legal drugs, such as aspirin, alcohol, and nicotine. Work as a class on the questionnaire. Compile your responses.

2. Keep a journal for one week. Write brief stories of triumph from those you find in the newspaper, in magazines, or on television.

3. Write your own story of triumph based on your life, or a story of triumph about someone in your family.

4. In the story "The Girl From Kiev," Rada uses her special skill in chess to overcome her fear of life in the United States. Write about special skills or talents that you may have. Can these skills and talents help you adjust to life in the United States?

5. Write about a famous person, such as José Feliciano, who is handicapped.

More Reading

Great Women In The Struggle: A Book of Black Heroes, Toyomi Ignus. Just Us Books, 1991.

Phillis Wheatley and Her Writings, William Robinson. Garland, 1984.

A Different Home, Tana Reiff. Fearon/Janus/Quercus, 1989.

Baseball in April and Other Stories, Gary Soto. Harcourt Brace Jovanovich, 1990.

The Story of Jackie Robinson, Bravest Man In Baseball, Margaret Davidson. Parachute Press, 1988.

Ahyoka and the Talking Leaves, Peter and Connie Roop. Lothrop, Lee, and Shepard, 1992.

Adopting Joe: A Black Vietnamese Child, Gretchen A. Duling. Charles E. Tuttle, 1977.

Bamboo and Butterflies: From Refugee to Citizen, J. D. Criddle. East/West Bridge Publishing House, 1992.

Through Moon and Stars and Night Skies, Ann Turner. Harper and Row, 1990.

Annie and the Old One, Miska Miles. Little, Brown, 1971.

Stories From Asia Today, A Collection for Young Readers, The Asian Cultural Center for UNESCO. Weatherhill/Heibonsha, 1976.

B-Ball: The Team That Never Lost a Game, Ron Jones. Bantam Books, 1990.

Hoang Breaks the Lucky Teapot, Rosemary Breckler. Houghton Mifflin, 1992.

Take a Walk in Their Shoes, Glennette Turner. Cobblehill Books, 1989.

Inspirations: Stories about Women Artists, Leslie Sills. A. Whitman, 1989.

Tales of the Earth

My forefathers taught me to reap and sow,
To take care of Mother Earth.
From her bosom we were brought,
And to her we shall all return.
So be humble, my brother,
And try to live in harmony.

Hamana
Cree Nation

The Lungs of the Earth
The Story of Chico Mendez

The rain forests of the world have been called the "lungs of the earth." They breathe in carbon dioxide and breathe out life-giving oxygen. They are the home for 70 percent of the plants used to fight cancer; one bird in three on earth nests in the rain forests. Yet, after existing for 70 million years, the rain forests are being destroyed. Since 1980, half of the rain forests (four million square miles) have been cut down and burned. Fifty million acres a year (96 acres a minute) are lost. By the year 2000, the beautiful rain forests of the world may be gone. In this true story, one man tries to save the rain forest and his childhood home.

Part 1

Chico Mendez was born in the rain forest of Brazil. He loved the beautiful birds, the huge green trees, the dragonflies, the soft rain that fell and fell. As a boy, he picked fruit and was never hungry. He chased the wild monkeys and caught beautiful butterflies. He climbed trees and swam in the clean rivers.

Chico's family were rubber tappers. For generations, the Mendez family had been rubber tappers. They drilled small, harmless holes into trees and drained the liquid that would become rubber. They sold the liquid to rubber companies and lived a simple life.

Then their life changed. Government men came one day. They said they were building roads into the rain forest, lots of roads. They were going to cut the trees down, millions of them, and sell the wood. Then they were going to build huge cattle ranches on the open land. The govern-

VOCABULARY

debt to owe money
awful terrifying
rattled shook
bulldozer large tractor
chain saw power saw used for cutting trees
in a flash in an instant
coughed expelled

ment needed money, they said. They were in debt. The people had to move. They had to leave their homes. They had to leave the rain forest where they had lived for generations.

The government paid the people money and many left. They didn't want to fight the government. But Chico Mendez refused to move.

"This is my home," he said. "I don't want to leave. My parents and my grandparents are buried here. My children are happy. Keep your money and go away."

But it didn't matter. One morning Chico heard a loud awful noise. It shook his body and rattled the peace of the rain forest. It was a bulldozer and it was pushing trees down and making a road. Men with chain saws were cutting down the huge beautiful trees. The saws buzzed like angry bees and in a few minutes, trees 80 years old were dead. The trees had given shade to Chico and his relatives for generations. The trees had been the home to beautiful birds and animals and insects for generations. Now, in a flash, they were gone. Forever.

The ugly bulldozers coughed brown smoke into the clean rain forest air. Other men drilled holes in the land looking for gold and oil. They used mercury to separate the gold from the rock and the mercury washed into the streams. Soon Chico saw dead fish and his family was afraid to drink the water anymore.

Part 2

Chico Mendez spoke with his friends. He told them to stay. One day Chico gathered 250 families and formed a human chain across the new road. The bulldozers stopped. The government workers cursed them. They called the police and the police beat Chico and his friends, but still they would not move. Work on the road slowed down.

Then Chico organized his friends. He formed a union, the Rural Workers' Union. For 13 years, Chico Mendez formed human chains. He organized 45 blockades. The government got tired. Some of the government workers went home. They liked Chico and didn't want to hurt him and his friends. Finally the gov-

VOCABULARY

curse swear
union organization of workers
explosion loud noise
shotgun powerful gun
wept cried

ernment of Brazil agreed to save part of the rain forest. They invited Chico to the capital city to talk with the government.

"If you destroy our home, people everywhere will suffer," Chico said. "The rain forest is only seven percent of the earth, but has half of all the living things. Do you want to destroy them? They are connected to other living things, like a long vine. Do you want to cut the vine? The monkeys are gone now and the dragonflies and the butterflies. What is the value of a butterfly? The butterfly is connected to something else and each has its purpose. Think of the medicine that comes from the plants and animals of the rain forest. Yet 17,000 living things a year are extinct from the cutting. Gone. Forever. After millions of years on this earth. I ask you again to stop the cutting."

Chico Mendez returned to the rain forest. He was more determined than ever to stop the destruction. But a man hated him. He was a rich cattle rancher. He formed his own union and said he would kill Chico.

Three days before Christmas, in 1988, there was an explosion in the rain forest. It was the sound of a shotgun. The blast hit Chico Mendez and he died. Chico had saved three million acres of rain forest. People said the green trees wept, and so did the butterflies that Chico loved. Even the sky poured down rain like tears to honor the man who tried to save the rain forest from destruction.

The Ozone Kid

Ozone is a layer of gas around the earth. It blocks the sun's harmful ultraviolet radiation from reaching the earth. Chemicals such as chlorofluorocarbons (CFCs), which are used in refrigeration, destroy ozone. Four billion tons of CFCs are released into the air each year. This has caused a dangerous thinning of the ozone layer. In this story, a Mexican boy plugs the hole in the ozone and saves the world.

Part 1

The year is 2050. The hole in the ozone is huge now. Ultraviolet light is flooding the earth. The plants are dying. Nobody can grow a garden anymore. No farms can grow food anymore. The world is dying from hunger.

Fifty million people each year are dying from skin cancer. The ozone is almost gone and there is little protection from the ultraviolet light. People wear sunglasses 24 hours a day, even when they sleep. They put sun block on their skin when they go outside so they don't get skin cancer. The only food comes from greenhouses protected from ultraviolet light.

Every rich family has a greenhouse. They grow enough food for their family, but for nobody else. Poor people, without greenhouses, die every day from hunger.

Some of the great teachers that rule the world—Buddha, Jesus, Mohammed, Confucius, Brahma, Krishna, Moses, medicine men and shamans—all sat down to talk. They were angry.

"What should we do about this?" one asked.

VOCABULARY

ozone a gas
ultraviolet light dangerous light from the sun
flooding overflowing
greenhouse a house of glass used to grow plants
filthy dirty
stink smell
smog smoky, foggy air

"Nothing," another one said. "We warned them. Didn't we tell them to shut off their air conditioners?"

"Yes. And now they're crying. Let them sweat, I say. Look at that filthy planet below us. Do you remember when the rivers were clean and the air was pure? I never want to go there anymore. My clothes stink from the smoke. My hair stinks."

"A few more years and they'll all be dead. Then we can start over."

But an old medicine man scratched his head. He was more patient. "Wait a minute," he said. "Let's save them one more time, but let's have some fun. You know that boy, Hector Torres?"

"The one who's always in trouble in school?"

"Yes."

"The one who's always chewing bubble gum in class?"

"That's the one."

"I don't like him. He doesn't listen to his mother."

"And he lives in Mexico City, doesn't he? I'm not going there. The smog is too bad. But what's your idea?"

"We'll have a worldwide contest," the medicine man said. "We'll give a billion dollars to the person who can fix the hole in the ozone. All the scientists think they're so smart. I'll fix it so Hector Torres wins. That's part of the problem on earth. The scientists think they know everything. They don't know anything. I want to teach them a lesson. I'll take the body of a poor beggar and fix everything."

Part 2

So it was agreed. The great teachers all said good-bye to the patient medicine man. They were sad to see him go. All of them had visited earth. They had all been killed or beaten by the people on earth and they didn't want this to happen to the medicine man.

The medicine man, however, was no fool. He didn't want to be beaten, either. So he looked down on the streets of Mexico City and found a wretched beggar. The man had sores all over his body and only one leg.

"Nobody will recognize me in that body," he said. So he made a deal with the man to use his body for three weeks.

A great contest was declared: "A BILLION DOLLARS TO ANY-ONE WHO CAN FIX THE HOLE IN THE OZONE!" The world buzzed. Everyone wanted the money. The scientists worked day and night. They sent airplanes into the hole with chemicals, but nothing worked.

Then one day the old medicine man lay on the street. Hector Torres walked by.

"Boy," the medicine man said, "A glass of water for the poor?" Hector Torres didn't answer. "Take this," the medicine man said, giving Hector a piece of bubble gum. "Bubble gum for a glass of water?"

Hector Torres brought the old medicine man water. Then he unwrapped the gum.

"That's good gum," Hector said. "That's the best I've ever had."

"And you've had a lot, too," the medicine man said.

"What?" Hector said.

"You've chewed a lot of bubble gum," the medicine man said. "But you're terrible at blowing bubbles."

"I am not," Hector said. "Watch this." Hector put his tongue into the gum and formed a bubble. He blew and blew. The bubble got bigger and bigger. Then, to his horror, he couldn't stop it. It grew to the size of a car. Then to the size of a house. Then it lifted him into the air like a huge balloon, and he went up and up. His lips were stuck to it. Higher and higher he went. Mexico City was a dot below him.

"I'll never chew gum in class again," he said. "I promise. I'll be good. I'll listen to my mother. Just don't let me fall."

Then the bubble popped in a huge explosion. The sound was heard all over the world. Windows broke in China. The huge sticky bubble made a perfect seal over the hole in the ozone and plugged it for good.

Hector drifted down to earth. He was a hero. He was rich. He was a billionaire. Everyone wanted some bubble gum, but he didn't have any more. Finally nobody believed his story.

Later Hector Torres went back to find the old beggar.

"I want some more bubble gum," Hector said.

The old beggar looked at him. "I've never seen you before, boy," he hissed. "Leave me alone."

VOCABULARY

no fool   not stupid
wretched   very poor
made a deal   made an
   agreement
seal   a cover
plugged   filled

The Hands of a Potter

Why would someone who loved to talk so much live alone in the woods in such an unusual house? The boy in this story meets someone different and he never forgets him.

When I was a boy, I knew a potter. He was from Japan. We were just kids, then, and of course we had a funny name for everybody. Well, we called him "the garbage man" because he lived on garbage. I don't mean garbage garbage, like food. He didn't eat food out of garbage cans. I mean he lived on things that other people threw away.

First, I'll tell you about his house. He lived in a tree house. That's right, he lived in a tree house and he never used a nail because he said he didn't want to hurt the tree, and all the wood for the house, even the windows, was scraps. It was all wood and windows that people had thrown out. But the way he did it, the way he built things, his house looked nice.

Like I said, he never used nails. He had the whole house tied to the tree with ropes, and wherever the house rubbed against the tree he put a piece of rubber from an old tire because he didn't want to hurt the tree. So whenever the wind blew, his whole house moved. That's why we never visited him on a windy day.

Now, to get up to his house you had to climb a rope ladder. But it was worth it because he lived different. First of all, he ate grass. Well, to us it was grass, but really it was plants that he picked in the woods. Sometimes he squeezed the plants in a press and drank the juice, especially wheat grass juice. He loved wheat grass juice.

He didn't have much furniture, either, just a few simple things that he made by himself, but they were nice. They were made of

VOCABULARY

scraps small pieces thrown out
press used to squeeze juice
mat a thin mattress
potter's wheel used to make pottery
kiln furnace
weird strange
interrupt not let someone finish speaking

wood from the forest and he covered them with cloth people had thrown away. At night he slept on a mat on the floor. During the day he rolled the mat up, so he didn't need a bedroom.

His tree house was full of plants. The sun came in all the windows and warmed the plants. He had a little deck on the outside of the house up in the trees and we liked to sit there. Everywhere you looked you saw plants. There were plants in the windows, plants hanging everywhere, and he knew everything about plants. You could ask him anything about plants and he would give you an answer.

"Dandelions? A blood purifier, son."

He always called us "son." He never knew our names.

And books were the other thing he liked. All the walls had bookshelves. His place was like a library, but I hardly ever saw him reading anything. I don't know when he read because he was too busy walking around the woods or making his pottery.

He had a little shop, a shed, for his pottery. He built the shop himself. Inside was his potter's wheel, a kiln to harden the clay, and shelves for the finished cups and plates.

People came by all the time to buy his pottery. Sometimes they didn't have much money and they paid him with food or with pictures they had painted. One person gave him a stained glass window and he put it in his tree house.

Sometimes people came by for his plants. Usually they were sick or somebody they knew was sick and he gave them plants. Sometimes he looked at their tongue and told them to stop eating.

He loved to talk. I could never figure out how somebody who loved to talk so much could live alone, but he did. He talked to everybody, about all kinds of things. One day a whole group of them was talking about needs versus desires. I couldn't understand it. I just remember they kept saying there was a difference.

I used to just hang around his place. He didn't mind. I loved to watch his hands when he made pots. He had amazing hands. He had long strong fingers. He would take a lump of wet clay, spin it on the wheel, and then form it into a ball. It looked so easy when he did it, but I tried it one day and I couldn't do it. And when he worked the clay his hands would change. They got soft and delicate like a piano player and he would put his thumbs into the center of the clay and make a pot or a cup or a plate. The clay would follow his delicate fingers up, up until the ball turned into a vase or a jar.

Now the thing is, he wasn't weird. I know he lived different, I mean in a tree house and all, but he wasn't weird. Everybody liked him. I never heard him raise his voice, or even interrupt anyone when they were speaking. He just liked to live alone in the woods in a tree house.

One day we moved away and I never saw him again. I'll never forget him. I think a lot of the things he talked about were true.

Flowers and Dreams

The Story of Rachel Carson

In 1951, the United States produced 275 million tons of pesticide, enough to kill 15 billion people, or six times the population of the earth. Many of these poisons harmed beautiful living things such as the peregrine falcon, fish, and songbirds. One shy woman who loved flowers dreamed of a world free of pesticide poisons and had the courage to write about it.

Part I

Few people change history. Rachel Carson did. Her book, *Silent Spring,* warned about pesticides in our environment. She said we were poisoning the earth.

Rachel was born in 1907 and grew up on a farm. She loved flowers and nature and took long walks with her dog, Candy, in the woods. Often she dreamed of becoming a writer. Her first story was published in a children's magazine when she was only ten years old.

Rachel first studied biology in college. She loved it so much that she took other science classes. Soon she changed her major from English to science. Her dream now was to become both a scientist *and* a writer.

In 1928, Rachel graduated from Chatham College. She finished her Master's Degree and taught zoology at Johns Hopkins University and the University of Maryland. Each summer, however, she left her teaching and visited the Woods Hole Marine Biological Laboratory in Massachusetts. There she studied the sea.

Rachel loved the waves, the salt air, the sea gulls, and the tide

VOCABULARY

pesticides poisons used to kill weeds and insects
environment the world around us
marine biological laboratory a place for studying the ocean
scripts stories

pools so much that she was inspired to write articles about the sea. She wrote in story form, mixing beautiful language with scientific facts.

In 1936, the Bureau of Fisheries in Washington, D.C. needed someone to write short radio stories about the sea. They needed someone who was both a scientist *and* a writer. They hired Rachel Carson.

Part 2

Soon there was a full-time position as a marine biologist at the Bureau of Fisheries. Rachel Carson applied and she was hired. She was only the second woman ever hired by the Bureau of Fisheries.

Part of her new work was to write booklets and articles for the Bureau of Fisheries. Her supervisor liked her writing. He encouraged Rachel to send an article to *Atlantic Monthly* magazine for publication.

The *Atlantic Monthly* was an important magazine. Rachel didn't believe they would publish her article. But in September, 1937, Rachel Carson's article, "Undersea," appeared in *Atlantic Monthly*. Rachel mixed beautiful language with scientific facts. This would become the trademark of her writing.

"The ocean is the place of paradoxes," she wrote. "It is the home of the great white shark, two thousand pound killer of the sea, and also the home of living things so small that your two hands might scoop up as many of them as there are stars in the Milky Way."

Important people saw her article and offered Rachel a book contract. In 1941, Rachel published *Under The Sea Wind,* her first book about sea life. Scientists praised her knowledge of science. But the book was also full of beautiful language. Often Rachel wrote as if she were under the water herself. She presented ocean life in a fresh, powerful, poetic manner. The United States, however, had just entered World War II and Rachel's book, though beautifully written, sold poorly and soon was forgotten.

VOCABULARY

marine biologist   someone who studies nature
supervisor   boss
trademark of her writing   her writing style
paradoxes   opposites
Milky Way   our galaxy

Rachel was not disturbed by poor sales of her book. She continued to write articles and study the sea. In 1952, she published *The Sea Around Us.* This book was an immediate success. It was on *The New York Times* best-seller list for 81 weeks. It received a National Book Award and was translated into 32 languages.

People around the world wanted to read Rachel's books now. Her first book was reprinted. Both of her books made the best-seller list at the same time. Rachel Carson was suddenly famous.

Part 3

Rachel Carson, however, had bigger dreams than fame and money. She dreamed about a clean, safe world for our children and our children's children, not a world poisoned with pollution and pesticides.

In 1958, she received a letter from a friend that worried her.

"The mosquito control airplane flew over our small town again. Our yard was sprayed since we are close to the marsh. The 'harmless' shower killed seven of our songbirds immediately. Three more were dead the next day. We scrubbed the bird bath but you can never kill DDT."

For a full year, Rachel read scientific reports about DDT and other pesticides. In one study, 71,430 fish died when pesticide sprayed from an airplane washed into a river. Only one and one-half pints of pesticide was used per acre. Rachel was so shocked by her research that she began writing a book about pesticide overuse.

Weakened by cancer, saddened by the death of her mother, and burdened with other writing and speaking commitments, Rachel Carson wrote late into the night. She was convinced that people simply did not know about the horrible effects of powerful pesticides and she could not rest until the world understood the danger.

In 1962, her most famous book, *Silent Spring,* was published. Rachel Carson said we were killing many beautiful living things

VOCABULARY

mosquito control airplane   an airplane that dropped pesticide
marsh   an area of wet high grass
scrubbed   washed
DDT   a powerful poison used to kill insects
reverence for life   respect for life

with pesticides, especially DDT, and poisoning our planet. She said we had created such powerful poisons that the mistakes we make now will last forever. She said life on our planet faced possible extinction, that someday we may have a "silent spring" because the birds and other living things may all be dead.

This startling information from a famous writer was new to the people in the United States and to the United States government. Few people were aware of the danger of DDT and other pesticides to the environment. Most people thought pesticides were needed by farmers for successful crops.

Chemical companies who manufactured pesticides called Rachel Carson a hysterical woman. They spent millions of dollars trying to prove her book wrong. Rachel Carson, however, was so thorough with her facts and so powerful with her words that President Kennedy, law makers in Washington, D.C., and the American people believed her.

Rachel Carson spoke to Congress and laws were passed to protect the environment. The ecology movement was started to save the earth. DDT was banned. People in many different countries became aware of how easily the earth can be poisoned.

Rachel Carson died of cancer in 1964. She was only 56. She never married. She cared for her sick mother and many relatives who had no money. She couldn't kill anything. Whenever she did research, she returned the animals back to the sea, even the smallest crab and tiny algae.

Rachel dedicated *Silent Spring* to a doctor named Albert Schweitzer. She loved his concept of "reverence for life." Her love for the earth and for all living things changed the way people think in the United States and the world.

Our Land Will Last Forever

Our land is more valuable than your money.
It will last forever.
It will not even perish by the flames of fire.
As long as the sun shines, and the waters flow,
This land will be here to give life to men and animals.
We cannot sell the lives of men and animals.
Therefore, we cannot sell this land.
It was put here for us by the Great Spirit
And we cannot sell it because it does not belong to us.
You can count your money and burn it within the nod of a
    buffalo's head,
But only the Great Spirit can count the grains of sand
And the blades of grass on these plains.
As a present to you,
We will give you anything we have that you can take with you.
But the land, never.

Anonymous Blackfoot Chief, Native American

Responding to Reading

Sharing Ideas

1. What is pollution? Discuss the different ways we have harmed the earth (litter, air, water, toxic dump sites such as Love Canal). Make a list of pollution in your home, in your school, in your neighborhood. How does pollution affect you or people you know? (Do your eyes sting? Do you get sick? Is your water safe?) Here are ways we can help the earth:

- ▲ Plant a tree. Trees breathe carbon dioxide and reduce the greenhouse effect. If only 100,000 people planted one tree one time, one million pounds of carbon dioxide would be absorbed each year, starting in 2010.
- ▲ Organize a drive to recycle the Sunday paper. It takes 500,000 trees to supply the United States with the Sunday paper each week. By learning to recycle, we reduce the need to cut down trees. Does your school recycle paper or other products? How can you find out? Does your school use recycled products? How can you find out?
- ▲ Organize a group cleanup of a nearby park or playground.
- ▲ Create an informational display on pollution in your classroom. Include articles, books, pictures, and examples of pollution and how people are fighting it.

2. Organize a rain forest awareness week in your school.

- ▲ Draw a picture of the rain forest. Share it with the class What does the rain forest look like? sound like? smell like? Are you or your friends in the picture? If so, what are you doing?
- ▲ Determine which products may destroy rain forests (hamburgers made from rain forest beef, for example). Create and display posters showing alternate products that do not harm the rain forests.
- ▲ Create displays about the rain forest. Include articles, books, and pictures of the rain forest.

- Put on a play for your school about the rain forest.
- Hold a fundraiser and adopt an acre of rain forest. The money pays for the protection of the land for one year.
- Write articles for your school newspaper about saving the rain forest.
- Invite parents, friends, and relatives to see your work.

3. Find an article about the hole in the ozone in the newspaper or a magazine. Share it with the class.

4. The poem "Our Land Will Last Forever" presents Native American attitudes toward the earth. Talk about the way people of your culture view the earth and their relationship with the earth. Compare other cultures' views with your own.

5. Write and perform a play about Chico Mendez.

Writing About the Earth

1. What do you think the world will be like in 2050? Write about it.

2. How have we hurt the earth? Work with a friend and list the ways people have harmed the earth. Do you think the earth can be saved?

3. Imagine you are a visitor from another planet. Describe the earth as you see and experience it for the first time. You may visit as many places as you choose: cities, farms, rich countries, poor countries, mountains, rivers, oceans, families, schools, hospitals.

4. What is composting? Research and write about how to compost and the value of composting. Do we have to live on a farm to compost, or can it be done in the city?

5. Have a "Save The Earth" poster contest.

6. Many groups have formed to help save the earth. Write to them to find out what they do and how you can help. Some organizations are: International Children's Rain Forest Program, Rain Forest Action Network, The Cultural Survival Group, TreePeople, Worldwatch Institute, National Resources Defense Council, Greenpeace, and Friends of the Earth. You can get their addresses at your local library.

More Reading

Fifty Simple Things You Can Do To Save The Earth, the Earth Works Group. Earthworks Press, 1989.

The City Kid's Field Guide, Ethan Herberman. Simon and Schuster, 1989.

Good Planets Are Hard To Find, An Environmental Informational Guide for Kids, Roma Dehr and Ronald Bazar. Firefly Books, 1990.

Rachel Carson: Voice for the Earth, Ginger Wadsworth. Lerner Publications, 1992.

One Day In The Tropical Rain Forest, Jean Craighead George. Harper and Row, 1990.

The People, Native Americans: Thought and Feelings, Roger Hammer. The Place In The Woods, 1991.

My Home in Brazil, Donna Bailey and Anna Sproule. Steck-Vaughn, 1991.

The Sacred Harvest: Ojibway Wild Rice Gathering, Gordon Regguinti. Lerner Publications, 1992.

Brown Pelican at the Pond, Edward O'Reilly. Manzanita Press, 1979.

Earthmaker's Tales, North American Indian Stories About Earth Happenings, Gretchen Will Mayo. Walker and Company, 1989.

The Story Vine: A Source Book of Unusual and Easy-to-Tell Stories from Around the World, Anne Pellowski. Macmillan; Collier Macmillan, 1984.

Tales of Dreams

What is life?
It is the flash of a firefly in the night.
It is the breath of a buffalo in the winter time.
It is the little shadow which runs across the grass
and loses itself in the sunset.

Crowfoot
Cheyenne, Native American

The Dream Keeper

Somewhere inside your heart your dream lies waiting. If you are not sure how to find your dream, ask the Dream Keeper. Her heart is the sun. Her eyes are the stars. Her voice is the wind. And she will whisper your dream into your ear.

Once, long ago, there was a girl who could talk to the birds. When she was little, she was happy. She walked in the forest and played by the stream and never thought about her purpose in life. But as she grew older, she asked: Why am I here? Where am I going? Who am I?

But no one could answer these questions, so one day she walked into the forest. Maybe the birds will know, she thought. They are my friends and I will talk to them. Look at how they live. There is no hesitation in their flight. There is no hesitation in their song. Surely they know their purpose. Maybe they know mine, too.

She walked until she saw a beautiful eagle.

"Eagle," she asked, "What is your purpose?"

"To fly above the earth," the eagle replied. "From there I can see all things. Here is my feather. Fly with me."

Next she saw a hawk.

"Hawk," she asked, "What is your purpose?"

"To be a messenger," the hawk replied. "I bring news of things to come. Here is my feather. Listen for my call."

Then a tiny hummingbird flew by.

"Hummingbird," she asked, "What is your purpose?"

"To love the flowers," the hummingbird replied. "My wings are their music. Here is my feather. Hold it close to your heart."

Then she saw a graceful swan.

"Swan," she asked, "What is your purpose?"

"To live in beauty," the swan replied. "Though the water is muddy, I see only my reflection. Here is my feather. Live in peace."

The girl sat down next to a river. The sunlight warmed the water and it was beautiful, but she was sad.

"I know the purpose of all the birds," she said, "but what is my purpose?"

Then a dragonfly with wings like paper flew by. The dragonfly saw the girl was sad and wanted to help her.

"And you, dragonfly," the girl finally asked, "what is your purpose?"

"To help people find their dreams," the dragonfly replied.

"Help me, then," the girl said. "I wish to know my dream."

"You must visit the Dream Keeper," the dragonfly said. "She will tell you. She lives nearby."

The girl looked around. There was no path anywhere. There was no one calling her name. The only noise was the sound of the river going over the rocks.

"Where is her house?" the girl asked.

"The wind will tell you," the dragonfly replied. "Listen to the wind." Then the dragonfly flew away.

The girl stood up. She listened for the wind, but the air was still. Then a soft breeze blew in the trees and she followed the breeze into the forest. Finally the breeze stopped and the forest was still.

"Dream Keeper?" the girl asked softly. But there was only silence. Then the grass quivered and the leaves rustled and a voice as beautiful as spring whispered, "Ask your question."

"I know the purpose of all the birds," the girl said, "but what is my purpose?"

"To find your dream and follow it," the Dream Keeper replied.

"Then tell me my dream," the girl said. "You are the Dream Keeper."

"Come closer and I will whisper your dream into your ear. But you must be still. Listen. Listen. Hush."

The girl felt the breeze blow gently, gently, oh, so gently into her waiting, waiting ear, and with a smile she recognized now and forever the voice of the Dream Keeper. Then from within her own heart she heard the music of the hummingbird, and she saw the beauty of the swan in the water, and she heard the sharp call of the hawk, and she flew with the eagle high above the earth, and she knew her dream and she followed it and she was happy.

The Hmong Warrior

In this story, a Hmong soldier is unable to adjust to his new life in the United States. He dreams of returning home and recapturing his village. What skills are needed for life in the United States? Why is it difficult for some refugees to learn these skills?

Mr. Vu Xiong sits in his small apartment in St. Paul. Outside snow is falling. His wife is cooking in the kitchen. His children are in school learning English. Not much has changed for them. His wife cooked in Laos and took care of the children. His children were in school.

But everything has changed for him. He was a village chief in Laos, with power and respect, and now he is nothing. He tries to work, but he has no skills. *"Tsis yog nej txoj kev txawj.* Not your skills," he says. *"Tabsi kuv kuj muaj kev txawj.* But I have skills. *Kuv siv tsis tau tab si nws nrog kuv nyob mus ib txhis.* They are of no use here, but they are my life."

Yes, he has skills. He is a skilled guerrilla soldier. How many lives did he save? How many American pilots did he rescue? How many people did he hide from enemy soldiers? How many times did he find food for hungry people with just his knife? How many times were others lost in the jungle, but he wasn't? How many people did he help cross the Mekong River to safety, with nothing but string and twigs and what he could gather from the jungle?

Yes, he has skills. He is a skilled farmer. How many rice crops did he plant? How many cattle and pigs and chickens did he care for? Did his family ever go hungry? Did his village ever go hungry?

Yes, he has skills. He is a skilled village chief. How many arguments did he settle? How many families did he heal? How many young men and women did he counsel?

But now, none of that is any good. He can work at a fast food restaurant with giggling American teenagers. He can fish and be laughed at for catching carp. He can work nights in a factory, maybe.

Living in the United States is easy for his children. They go to school. They learn English. They learn many new things. They drive a car. They have freedom. They can't remember the old country.

Living in the United States is easy for his wife. She stays home. She cooks. She sews. She talks Hmong with her relatives.

But it is hard for him. His life is in the past.

Today, like other days, he dreams about the General and returning to Laos and recapturing his village. He hears there is a secret army in training, of Hmong freedom fighters, and he wants to join. He wants to become a man again and die as a man in the mountains of Laos near the village of his birth. That is his dream.

VOCABULARY

village chief   leader
guerrilla soldier   jungle fighter
pilots   people who fly airplanes
rescue   save
twigs   small branches

The United States is a slow death for him. He sits and watches the snow day after day. The frozen winter in St. Paul is like his life, dead and useless. His memories are frozen, like the cruel winter all around him, nothing alive anymore, everything dead. Day after day he sits and watches the snow and waits for news from the General.

A Story from Silver Lake

Life in a rest home was hard for Clara. But she loved Jim, another resident. Together they cared for each other. They were not lonely, like the others, because they had love. But one day things changed.

Part 1

The Silver Lake Rest Home was clean and quiet, but it was not a happy place. Old people, many forgotten, came here to die. Men and women sat slumped in chairs. Some talked to themselves, others talked out loud to anyone who would listen. Others had had strokes and couldn't talk at all.

Clara hated it. She was 83, but healthy and strong. Everyone around her complained. The food wasn't good enough. The care wasn't good enough. The nurses didn't come fast enough. They never had a good day. There was always something wrong.

VOCABULARY

stroke   a disease
complain   to not like something
avoid   stay away from
cherry cheesecake   a dessert in the United States

Clara avoided these people. She knew they were just lonely, but still she avoided them. Each day she woke up, got herself dressed, and went to see Jim.

Jim lived in a room down the hall. He seldom had visitors. His three children lived far away. His wife had died long ago. But Clara knew his heart, his gentleness, and she loved him very much.

"Good morning, dear," she said, fixing his pillow and straightening his room. "How did you sleep?"

"Fine," Jim said. He never complained.

"What did you dream about last night?"

"The Christmas my mother baked cherry cheesecake," Jim said, "I was only ten. Isn't it something, Clara?"

"How we can remember things from long ago?"

"Yes," Jim said, "That was 75 years ago."

"I know," Clara said, pouring their coffee. "I have a hard time remembering what I did yesterday, but I can remember things from years ago."

They sat together at a small table in Jim's room, next to the window. On the windowsill were pictures of Jim's three children and his 12 grandchildren.

"It's happening every night now, Clara," Jim said, "The dreams, I mean. Do you think it means anything?"

"I don't know, dear," Clara said.

"They're so clear," Jim said. "They're just like a movie. And they're always about things long ago, when I was a boy. I remember the kids in school and our family home and my neighborhood, and it's just like it happened yesterday."

"Are your dreams in color, too, Jim?"

"Yes," Jim said.

"Mine, too," Clara said, "Beautiful color. It's all so lovely."

"But they're happening every night now, Clara. That's the strange thing. It never used to be this way. Do you think it means anything?"

"I don't know," Clara said again, looking into Jim's puzzled eyes.

Part 2

Together Jim and Clara had their morning coffee, like they always did. They sat by the window in the sunlight. There was a bird feeder in the snow.

"The cardinals are hungry today," Clara said, sipping her coffee. "Such a lovely red against the snow. And the chickadees are so polite, aren't they Jim? Look at how they wait for each other."

Jim was silent.

His soft hands were on his coffee cup. His kind eyes were still puzzled, searching for an answer to his dreams. When he spoke again, he looked at Clara, hesitating for a moment, fearful at what she might say.

"Last night my mother spoke to me, Clara," he said, expecting Clara to say something disbelieving.

But nothing moved on Clara's face.

"I didn't imagine it, Clara," he said, still expecting her not to believe him.

Clara's fingers moved nervously on her coffee cup. A light snowfall had started outside the window. The flakes were beautiful, soft as cotton against the blue sky. They landed gently on the green trees and glistened like diamonds in the sunlight.

"Those nasty blue jays," Clara finally said, "Look at them spill that food on the ground."

"You don't believe me, do you?" Jim said, looking away.

"I didn't say that, Jim."

"You don't believe me. You think I'm making this up. But I'm not. She didn't speak to me like you and I do. She was just there, Clara, and I knew what she was thinking."

Clara got up from the table. She walked around Jim's room and busied herself with lots of little things. She dusted his reading table. She cleaned his mirror. She watered his plants. She fluffed his pillow. She washed his favorite cup. She folded his laundry. She turned the radio on to his favorite station.

But then she turned the radio off. The music bothered her. She looked at Jim sitting by the window. His soft hands were still on his coffee cup. His soft eyes were still puzzled. His long arms were still graceful, even in old age.

Finally she walked over to him and put her arms around him.

"Would you like to play cards, dear?" she said softly, laying a deck of playing cards on the table by the window.

"She was just there, Clara," Jim said slowly. "I know it's hard to believe, but it's true. It was like a dream, but it wasn't a dream. And I knew what she was thinking. And she knew what I was thinking. That's how we spoke to each other. It wasn't with words. And her world was just as real to me as this world. And I'm so tired today, Clara, I'm so tired. I hardly know what day it is anymore, and I can't think straight anymore, and names and people and places and things are all blurred. It's like there are two worlds for me now, this one here where you and I live which is fading away, and that one at night in my dreams, which is sharp and clear, and I don't know which one is real, Clara. I don't know anymore. I'm just so tired all the time now."

Clara took Jim's hand. She touched his face.

"I believe you, Jim," she whispered, "I really do."

Then she stood up and looked out the window. "I just don't want you to go, yet, Jim."

"There's nothing to be afraid of, Clara. I know that now. There's love here and there's love there."

"I know," Clara whispered, "I know."

Outside the window, children played in the snow. Clara heard their laughing voices. They ran and played and threw snow at each other, the way Clara had done as a child, and Jim, too, so many years ago. All of that seemed like a blink in time now. Behind the children the beautiful sky was blue and clear, like the sky in Jim's dreams. The snowflakes settled on the pine trees and turned the trees from green to dazzling white.

"What a lovely snowfall," Clara said, "As clear and beautiful as your dreams, Jim."

Jim didn't answer, nor did Clara expect an answer. His head was on his chest. His eyes were closed. His face was still. His graceful arms were silent. His soft hands still hugged his warm coffee cup.

"Good-bye, Jim," Clara whispered. "I love you, dear."

The Woman Who Dreamed of Freedom

The Story of Harriet Tubman

In this true story, a black slave dreams of freedom. One night she runs away and follows the North Star to freedom. But can she rescue her friends still in slavery in the South?

Once there was a woman who dreamed of freedom. She was a black slave named Harriet Tubman. She was born in 1820 on a plantation in Maryland. She dreamed of following the North Star to freedom in the northern states.

VOCABULARY

plantation large farm
northern states states without slavery
master white owner

Her childhood was hard. When Harriet was seven, she was sent away by her master, Edward Brodas, to care for the baby of a white woman. The woman gave Edward Brodas a small amount of money each week for Harriet. Little Harriet was put in a wagon, without saying good-bye to her mother and father, and taken away.

Harriet cleaned the house and cared for the woman's baby. The woman kept a whip and if the baby cried she whipped Harriet. Harriet was whipped so many times that she had scars on her neck for the rest of her life.

One day Harriet ran away. She was still a small girl. She was going to be whipped and she ran out the door and hid for four days. But she had to return because she had nothing to eat. The white woman was angry and brought Harriet back to Edward Brodas.

When Harriet was 11 she worked in the fields. She was strong. At night she listened to the slaves whisper about freedom. There was something called "the Underground Railroad." It was a series of secret roads and trails that led north to freedom. Some white people hated slavery and they hid slaves on the Underground Railroad. Their houses were called "stations." The white people who lived in these houses were called "station masters." People who came south and led slaves north to freedom were called "conductors."

As Harriet listened to slaves talk about the Underground Railroad, her dream of freedom grew stronger. She wanted to follow the North Star out of slavery, even as a young girl.

One day Harriet saw a fight. A white man was whipping his slave and Harriet stepped between them. The slave ran out the door and the white man threw a heavy iron weight at the slave. The iron weight missed the man and hit Harriet in the head. She almost died. For the rest of her life she had sleeping spells, headaches, and a deep scar on her head.

When Harriet got older she married John Tubman, a free black man. She told him that she wanted to be free, too. She told him she dreamed at night about crossing a great line. On one side was slavery, on the other side was freedom.

One day Harriet heard she was going to be sold. That night she left for freedom without saying good-bye to anyone. She followed the North Star, walking through woods and swamps at night and hiding during the day. Many white people along the Underground Railroad helped her.

She walked all the way to Pennsylvania and freedom. But she thought about her family and friends still in slavery in the South. She decided to become a conductor on the Underground Railroad. She walked back and forth many times, taking small groups of slaves to freedom. In all she helped 300 slaves reach freedom in the North. At one point, there was a $40,000 reward offered for her, dead or alive.

The slaves called Harriet "Black Moses" and waited in their small log cabins for her to rescue them. She was never caught, although many times she was close to being discovered.

After the Civil War, slavery ended in the United States. Harriet Tubman lived in Auburn, New York. She started a home for the poor. She was famous now. Thousands of people wrote letters to her. The Queen of England wanted to meet her.

Harriet Tubman, however, continued to live a simple life. She cared for the poor until she died in 1913 at the age of 90. Her dream of freedom had come true for herself and others.

Memories of a Man

Once the Lakota people lived on the land that is now the United States. Their culture was closely connected to the earth. They taught their children that the earth was their mother and that they were caretakers of the earth. In this story, a young Lakota boy grows old and watches his world vanish.

Part 1

Long ago, Grey Eagle lived on the Great Plains. He was a boy, then. The sun was warm on his brown body and he lived with the rest of the Lakota nation. He chased rabbits under the open sky. He ran through the prairie grass with his friend, Little Bear. He rode his horse like the wind and chased buffalo too many to count.

The days passed quickly. Mother Earth was kind. The summer storms were tender. The winter months were warm. The sun rose and fell like a lullaby. His people camped in the Sacred Hills during the snows of winter and his father told him stories.

VOCABULARY

lullaby   song
Sacred Hills   the Black Hills
quivering grass   grass blown by
   the wind
eternal   forever

"*Wambli Hota.* Grey Eagle," his father said. "What story do you want tonight?"

"Tell me the story of Bright Star and how he fought the North Wind!" Grey Eagle said, moving closer to the fire and pulling his buffalo blanket around his body.

"Bright Star?" his father said, pleased with his son's choice. "Bright Star was the child of a beautiful Lakota woman and the morning star. He fought for us against Wazeeyah, the North Wind. Once, there was a terrible battle. Both were tired. Bright Star fanned himself with eagle feathers. The wind from the eagle feathers melted the snow of Wazeeyah and he was angry. They stopped fighting forever. Now Wazeeyah controls only half the year with his snow. Each spring, Bright Star fans the skies with his eagle feathers and the warm wind melts the snow again."

Grey Eagle loved his father's voice. His father taught him about the Lakota people and their love for the earth.

"The land belongs to Wakan-Tanka and the Great Elders," his father said. "It belongs to the sun, the wind, and the rain and no one can claim it." Grey Eagle learned of the great circle and the oneness of all things: the morning mist, the quivering grass, the delicate butterfly, the floating eagle. Death was the end of nothing. Life went on. The soul of the Lakota was eternal.

Part 2

When spring came, Grey Eagle left the Sacred Hills with his family. Now his father taught him to hunt.

"*Chinkish, tayan anagoptan yo.* Today, I want you to *really* look and listen," his father said. "Tonight I will ask you questions."

At night his father was serious.

"Where were the fish in the stream today? Which direction was the wind? When will the red berries be ripe? Where is the main buffalo herd? What songbirds did you hear? Where are their nests? You must know these things. Someday you must provide for your people."

VOCABULARY

serious not joking
ripe ready to eat
herd group of animals
provide for take care of

In the summer months, Grey Eagle hunted buffalo with his father. He rode his horse and painted his face. He shot his arrows and danced at night.

He grew tall and strong. His father, his mother, his uncles and aunts, his grandparents, and the Lakota elders loved him. The sun was warm on his life. The grass was green and sweet. The rivers were full of fish. The buffalo were beyond count.

Part 3

Then one day his father spoke about the white man. His father's face was angry. White people were crossing Lakota land in covered wagons. The buffalo were dying, shot for their hides, or their heads, or for no reason. Grey Eagle heard stories of the cruelty to his people at Sand Creek and Washita. His father's face was cold.

VOCABULARY

Sand Creek and Washita
  massacre sites
yellow metal gold
fire sticks guns
sweat lodge sauna
drought no water
famine no food

"They buy and sell with the yellow metal," his father said. "The yellow metal drives them crazy. And they have fire sticks to kill the buffalo. The buffalo are dying. They let them rot on the prairie. Soon we will starve." There was sadness in his father's voice.

Then one day, his father said, "Son, it is time for you to seek your vision. Go to the Sacred Hills. You must understand the white man."

Grey Eagle blackened his face with burnt wood. He rode his pony into the hills and found a beautiful hill overlooking the Lakota land. He heated rocks and cleansed himself in a sweat lodge ceremony. Then he began his fast, his *hambleca*.

Each day, he asked for a vision. It was in the Moon of the Strawberries, when the buffalo were fighting and the streams swollen with fish.

On the third day, his vision came. In his vision, he saw that great sorrow was coming to the Lakota people. The nation would die, crushed by the westward movement of white people.

This is what Grey Eagle saw:

He saw a fire stick and a spear. This was war with the whites. The rivers were red with blood. The songbirds were silent, replaced with screams of the dying. The spear of the Lakota was broken.

The grass turned brown. This was drought and famine. The buffalo were dead. Their bones were everywhere. Indian people were cold and hungry. Their contact with the earth and their past was broken and forgotten.

Then Grey Eagle was on a high mountain. Two Spirit Warriors pointed to the future, many years away. The Lakota nation was reborn. It was one hoop among many. All the hoops of the world were joined in a big circle. In the center of the circle, the spirit tree bloomed and there was peace.

When Grey Eagle awoke from his vision, he was sad. His tears fell on the sand. He knew war was coming and life as he knew it would die.

Part 4

When Grey Eagle returned to the village, he shared his vision with his sponsor, a *Wechasha Wakan*, a Holy Man. Then each day he watched the white people. Little by little, his vision came true.

War broke out between the soldiers and the Lakota. The Lakota were overpowered. They joined with the Cheyenne and drove the soldiers away. But the soldiers returned and finally a peace treaty was signed. In the agreement, the Sacred Hills belonged to the Lakota forever.

Then gold was found in the hills and the soldiers returned to take the sacred land from the Lakota people. This time the number of soldiers and their power was crushing. There was a bitter war. Thousands died.

VOCABULARY

palsy shaking
the ways the culture, the traditions
grotesque ugly

A cruel winter came. The Lakota had little food or clothing. The buffalo were gone and they faced certain starvation. They surrendered, except for Crazy Horse and those with him. Finally, weak and exhausted, they too gave up. Within days, Crazy Horse was dead. A soldier stabbed him with a bayonet and he bled to death.

The soldiers ordered the Lakota people to live on reservations. The Lakota lived in square houses now, not round teepees. They were cold and hungry and dying. Finally, a small group of desperate Lakota gathered for the Ghost Dance. They wanted to bring the buffalo back so they could eat. They wanted the white people to go away.

Soldiers came to stop the Ghost Dance. Many of the Lakota people left the reservation in fear. They camped at Wounded Knee Creek and planned to return to the reservation the next day.

Grey Eagle was with the starving Indians at Wounded Knee Creek. It was winter. They were cold. Everyone he passed was sick and hungry and dressed in rags. His eyes filled with tears at the suffering of his people.

"Woman," he whispered, bending down to help a mother and her small child, "is there no food?"

"Nothing," she said. The snow and cold rattled her lips.

"Cover your child with this blanket from my horse," Grey Eagle said, "I will walk to the fires and return with food."

But Grey Eagle never reached the fires at Wounded Knee. Someone fired a gunshot. Then there was an explosion of gunfire. The horrible sound shook the Sacred Hills and lasted forever. The screams were terrible and Grey Eagle watched his people die like cattle.

Palsy shook Grey Eagle's body and he fell unconscious in the snow. Another vision came to him. Two Spirit Warriors took him into the sky. They sat him down in front of six elders. Grey Eagle flooded their feet with tears.

"Grey Eagle," the elders said. "The sky, the wind, the rain, the morning sun, weep for our people today. But you have been spared. A young boy will come to you in your old age. Teach him the ways of the Lakota people. The spiritual heartbeat of our people must not be lost during this time of sorrow. Go now. Keep the ways. Help your people."

When Grey Eagle awoke, the bodies of Sioux men, women, and children lay frozen in death. Chief Big Foot was dead. His body was frozen into a grotesque shape in the winter snow. Unable to look at his people any longer, Grey Eagle walked to the reservation and surrendered.

Part 5

Years went by. The Lakota people ate government food. Sometimes it came; sometimes it didn't. Lakota children were taken away from their parents. They were sent to government schools at a young age and beaten if they spoke their own language or practiced their own customs.

Grey Eagle lived in a small house on the reservation. He was very old now. He spoke to no one. He decided to remain silent until his death. He was forbidden to practice the sacred ceremonies of his people and he had nothing to say to anyone.

Then one summer, long after Grey Eagle had forgotten his vision at Wounded Knee, a young Indian boy came down the dirt road of the reservation.

"*Tunkashila*. Grandfather," he said politely, walking up to Grey Eagle, "I'm looking for an old man named Grey Eagle. Do you know him?"

"Why do you ask?" Grey Eagle said, looking into the boy's face.

"Because I had a dream," the boy said. "In my dream, two Spirit Warriors came to me and carried me on a cloud into the sky. They sat me down in front of six elders in a beautiful teepee. They told me to leave the city and find Grey Eagle. They said this man would teach me the ways of the Lakota people."

A distant memory stirred in Grey Eagle's tired mind. He stood and looked down the long dirt road of the reservation toward the distant hills barely visible on the horizon.

"Son," he said slowly, "Is this not the Moon of the Strawberries? Are not the buffalo fighting and the streams swollen with fish?"

"I don't know," the boy replied.

"Of course not," Grey Eagle said.

Then Grey Eagle remembered the vision the elders had given him long ago at Wounded Knee. He looked at the boy again. Was this the spirit boy?

Then the boy took a knife from his pocket and cut his finger.

"*Tunkashila*. Grandfather," the boy said. "Here is my blood."

Tears streamed down Grey Eagle's old face. Surely this was the boy the elders had promised.

"Come to me, my beloved son," Grey Eagle said, placing his old hands on the boy's shoulders. "I am Grey Eagle and I have many things to teach you."

Part 6

For days and days, Grey Eagle taught the boy the ways of the Lakota people. He taught him about the sweat lodge, the sacred pipe, the beating of the drums, the eagle feathers, the power of the animals, and the healing plants. He taught the boy the Lakota stories, and the songs and dances of his people. Then Grey Eagle spoke about the vision quest.

"Seek your vision alone in silence," he said. "Ask to learn self-control, courage, patience, endurance, dignity, and reverence. Ask to be of service to your people. Ask that war and destruction may end."

The boy left. He rode alone toward the Sacred Hills, like Grey Eagle did years ago. He was alone, but strong, eager and confident. Grey Eagle had prepared him well. He was not afraid. He knew the Lakota elders loved him and would grant him a vision.

Old Grey Eagle watched the boy go. Finally, the boy was just a speck on the dirt road. Grey Eagle was happy. He knew the ways of the Lakota people would live on. The Elders make no mistakes. Surely this boy was the one.

Grey Eagle lay down on the wooden porch of his reservation house. He faced east and breathed his last breath. There was peace on his face and rest in his body. He knew for certain now that the ways of his people would return again, that the days of despair would someday end.

Far in the distance, the boy rode on toward the Sacred Hills. Overhead, in the clear summer sky, a magnificent eagle was soaring and waiting.

Responding to Reading

Sharing Ideas

1. The word "dreams" has many different meanings. It can mean dreams at night when you are sleeping. It can mean your hopes or aspirations for the future. It can mean visions, or seeing into the future. Discuss the following:

▲ Dreams during our sleep have been the object of fascination and study by many different cultures for thousands of years. What is the meaning of dreams? Why do we dream? Can dreams tell the future? What dreams have you had? Have you had any dreams of something that was going to happen in the future? Have you ever had recurring dreams?

147

flying dreams? dreams of being chased? falling dreams? Do you dream in black-and-white or color?

- ▲ What are your dreams for the future? What are your dreams for your children, or your friends, or your family?
- ▲ When you "dream" about the past, what do you think about? When you "daydream," what do you think about?
- ▲ Do you believe in visions? In the story "Memories of a Man," Grey Eagle has two visions. What were his visions? Can anyone have a vision?

2. The story "A Story from Silver Lake" is about a rest home. Some people go to a rest home when they are old. Do you think this is right? Should we take care of our parents when they are old? What if they are sick and we can't take care of them? Would you ever put your parents in a rest home?

3. What is the value of age? What do older people know that younger people do not? Can this knowledge be learned in school?

4. Discuss the role of the elderly in your culture and in other cultures. How do elderly people participate in the family? in the community? Where do they live? How are they cared for?

5. What was Harriet Tubman's dream? Did she realize her dream? What obstacles stood in her way?

6. Dr. Martin Luther King, Jr. gave a famous speech called "I Have a Dream." Listen to his speech, or have your teacher read the speech to you. What was his dream? Do you think his dream will come true?

Writing About Dreams

1. What dream do you have for your life?
- ▲ Write about where you would like to live (small town, big city, in the country).
- ▲ Describe your home, your family, your employment, and your general life-style.
- ▲ Describe your personal goals and achievements.

2. The man in the story "The Hmong Warrior" dreamed about the past. Why did he think about the past so much? Why was the present so painful for him, and his future in the United States so impossible? Write about your own past.

▲ Would you do anything differently, if given a chance? What would you change? Why? What happened? Who was there? How old were you? How would you "rewrite" what happened?

▲ What things are hard for you to forget? Why? What emotions are most difficult to forget or change?

3. Make a list of things you have learned from older people. Work with a friend. Think of your parents, relatives, teachers, and older friends. Think of:

▲ advice older people have given you,

▲ stories older people told to you with lessons about people and life,

▲ skills older people have taught you,

▲ knowledge gained from your teachers and older relatives.

▲ the many positive contributions that retired people are making to life in the United States.

4. Pretend you are talking to the Dream Keeper. Write down your conversation.

More Reading

Dream Catcher, Audrey Osofsky. Orchard Books, 1992.

Yagua Days, Cruz Martel. Dial Press, 1976.

A Picture Book of Harriet Tubman, David Adler. Holiday House, 1992.

The Most Beautiful Place in the World, Ann Cameron. Alfred A. Knopf, 1988.

When Clay Sings, Byrd Baylor. Charles Scribner's Sons, 1972.

Tortillitas Para Mamá and Other Spanish Rhymes, Margot Griego. Holt, Rinehart and Winston, 1981.

Walking the Road to Freedom, A Story about Sojourner Truth, Jeri Ferris. Carolrhoda Books, 1988.

First Snow, Helen Coutant. Knopf, 1974.

Buffalo Woman, Paul Goble. Macmillan, 1984.

Racing the Sun, Paul Pitts. Avon Books, 1988.

The Invisible Hunters, Harriet Rohmer. Children's Press, 1987.

The Tamarindo Puppy and Other Poems, Charlotte Pomerantz. Greenwillow Books, 1980.

Multicultural Index

Literary Genre Index

References

Abrahamson and Carter. *Books For You, A Booklist for Senior High Students.* Urbana, Illinois: National Council of Teachers of English, 1988.

Arbuthnot, May Hill. *Time for Fairy Tales, Old and New.* Chicago, Illinois: Scott Foresman and Company, 1961.

California State Department of Education. *Recommended Readings In Literature, K-8.* Sacramento, California, 1986.

DeStefano, Susan. *Chico Mendez: Fight for the Forest.* Twenty-First Century Books, 1992.

Educational posters from United Tribes Educational Technical Center, Bismarck, North Dakota.

Foster, Leila M. *The Story of Rachel Carson and the Environmental Movement.* Chicago, Illinois: Children's Press, 1990.

Greene, Carol. *Black Elk, A Man With A Vision.* Chicago, Illinois: Children's Press, 1990.

Hammer, Roger. *Hispanic America.* Golden Valley, Minnesota: The Place In The Woods, 1991.

Hammer, Roger: *The People, Native Americans: Thoughts and Feelings.* Golden Valley, Minnesota: The Place In The Woods, 1991.

Ignus, Toyomi. *Book of Black Heroes, Great Women In The Struggle.* Orange, New Jersey: Just Us Books, 1991.

Jagendorf, M.A. and R.S. Boggs. *The King of the Mountain: A Treasury of Latin American Folk Stories.* New York: The Vanguard Press, 1960.

McGovern, Ann. *Runaway Slave, The Story of Harriet Tubman.* New York: Four Winds Press, 1965.

Morey, Janet Nomura and Wendy Dunn. *Famous Asian Americans.* New York: Cobblehill Books, 1992.

Neihardt, John C. *Black Elk Speaks.* New York: W. Morrow and Company, 1932. Reprint. New York: Washington Square Press, 1959.

Nilsen, Alleen Pace. *Your Reading, A Booklist for Junior High and Middle School Students.* Urbana, Illinois: National Council of Teachers of English, 1991.

Ringquist, Lois. *Rainbow Collection, Multicultural Books for Older Children.* Minneapolis, Minnesota: Minneapolis Public Library and Information Center, 1991.

Ringquist, Lois. *Celebrate the Hispanic Experience in Children's Books.* Minneapolis, Minnesota: Minneapolis Public Library and Information Center, 1991.

Shaw, B. "Candle In The Wind." *People Weekly* 33 (April 23, 1990) 86–90.

Sterling, Philip. *Sea and Earth, The Life of Rachel Carson.* New York: Thomas Y. Crowell Company, 1970.

Smallwood, Betty Ansin. *The Literature Connection, A Read-Aloud Guide for Multicultural Classrooms.* Reading, Massachusetts: Addison-Wesley Publishing Company, 1991.

Terada, Alice. *Under the Starfruit Tree, Folktales from Vietnam.* Honolulu: A Kolowalu Book, University of Hawaii Press, 1989.

Wadsworth, Ginger. *Rachel Carson, Voice for the Earth.* Minneapolis, Minnesota: Lerner Publications, 1992.

Walker, Barbara. *The Dancing Palm Tree And Other Nigerian Folktales.* Lubbock, Texas: Texas Tech University Press, 1990.

White, Ryan. *Ryan White, My Own Story.* New York: Dial Books, 1991.

Wolkstein, Diane. *The Banza.* New York: The New Dial Press, 1981.